EDITED BY ALFRED E. MULDER

LEARNING
TO COUNT TO
ONE

THE JOY AND PAIN OF BECOMING A MULTIRACIAL CHURCH

FAITH
ALIVE®
Christian Resources

Grand Rapids, Michigan

Library of Congress Cataloging-in-Publication Data

Learning to count to one : the joy and pain of becoming a multiracial church / edited by Al Mulder.
    p. cm.
  ISBN 1-59255-296-X
  1. Race relations--Religious aspects--Christian Reformed Church. 2. Christian Reformed Church--History. 1. Mulder, Al.
  BT734.2.L35 2006
  285.7'31089--dc22

                2005035469

10 9 8 7 6 5 4 3 2 1

CONTENTS

FOREWORD

Learning to Count to One is a timely treatment of an important topic. As the Christian Reformed Church (CRC) approaches her sesquicentennial (150th) year in 2007, it is appropriate that she reflect on her journey from having a mostly monoethnic heritage to increasingly becoming a multiethnic community of faith. This discussion is not new, nor is it finished. The discussion is happening globally in the World Alliance of Reformed Churches; *Learning to Count to One* is our contribution to that broader discussion.

Alfred E. Mulder has devoted most of his ministry to understanding and celebrating the richness of cultural diversity among the people of God. He has done so in the practice of ministry, in the writing of songs, in countless meetings, and in taking on this project as editor of *Learning to Count to One*. To Al, and to all who contributed to this discussion, we are deeply grateful. May the discussion be enriched by these reflections, and may the vision of saints ransomed for God "from every tribe and language and people and nation" (Rev. 5:9) be increasingly evident in the Church everywhere.

—Peter Borgdorff

Executive Director
Christian Reformed Church in North America

September 2005

INTRODUCTION

"So in Christ we who are many form one body, and each member belongs to all the others." —Romans 12:5

I was born on a farm in northwest Iowa. My great-great-grandfather, Yge Mulder, immigrated to Sioux County from the Netherlands in 1868. Some thirty years later my mother's father emigrated from the same Dutch village. In my childhood, as far as I know, every known living relative was Dutch American. Every student at my country school was Dutch American. Every farmer in our threshing ring was of Dutch descent. So was every member in our congregation. So were all my teachers, from grade school through high school.

The only folks I can remember who were not Dutch were the undertaker for my brother's funeral and a young vacation Bible school teacher who led me to commit my life to Christ. Although not "Dutch," even they were white like me. As a child, my world was all white.

The author, second of ten children, is seated to the left. Gerald, the firstborn, was fatally injured in a farm accident at age eleven. Younger brother Harold is a retired educator.

What a difference a half-century makes! I still am white and of Dutch descent. But if you were to hang around with me awhile, you would notice that my racial and cultural circle has become more diverse. Our home is decorated with southwestern art. Our gallery of grandchildren includes faces with Hispanic and Navajo features. Our resident grandson is a "white kid" on a mostly black football team. Our first great-grandson has African curls. The supermarket where we shop has the look and feel of an international market. The congregation I belong to is African American, Asian American, Hispanic, and white. In God's kind providence, I am *learning to count to one.*

I first heard the phrase *Learning to Count to One* in Kalamazoo, Michigan. The Rev. Denise Posie pastors a multiracial congregation there. At the celebration of her fifth anniversary at Immanuel CRC, the Rev. Dr. J. Louis Felton of nearby Galilee Missionary Baptist Church spoke on *Learning to Count to One.* I express my deep thanks to Dr. Felton for generously granting permission for me to use his phrase in this book.

WHY THIS BOOK?

This also is the growing story of the Christian Reformed Church. The CRC numbers approximately one thousand congregations, three-fourths of them in the United States and one-fourth in Canada. Since the beginning of my ministry in 1960, I have witnessed increasing racial and cultural diversity on several fronts in my originally Dutch immigrant denomination. So I am grateful for the opportunity to trace the story of this increasing diversity in the CRC—as hesitant and halting as it has been. To echo my grandson Al Garcia about his experience in the 101st Airborne, "I think I was born for this."

This project was first posed by CRC executive director Rev. Peter Borgdorff. As a delegate to the World Alliance of Reformed Churches, Borgdorff was monitoring a unique initiative to explore the relationship between so-called mainline churches and immigrant churches.

In 1999 the World Alliance of Reformed Churches and John Knox Reformed International Centre began joint sponsorship of Mission in Unity, with Jet den Hollander as project director.

This prompted him to suggest that the CRC contribute a case study of its own journey as a historically immigrant denomination. As we began imagining this study, another important objective emerged. Because the CRC is committed to becoming a more racially diverse and reconciled family of churches, we became convinced that this study also would enhance this important vision and goal.

What's the Difference?

In preparation for this project, I was privileged to meet with Dutch leaders who had already submitted a study.

I discovered that the Dutch are dealing with issues and concerns that are similar to those in North America—issues like the social and economic plight of immigrants, especially those from Africa, Asia, and the Middle East, as well as the attending mission opportunities and challenges. Another similarity is that the CRC and the Protestant Church in the Netherlands (PCN) are both motivated by the mission of God and by our common identity in Christ.

There also are important differences between the two denominations. In the Netherlands, immigrant Christians formed congregations that are organizationally separate, leaving the PCN membership almost exclusively white. According to Dr. Sjaak van't Kruis, "It is not only remarkable but also disquieting that things remain so 'white'" within the established Dutch churches" (*Born in Zion,* p. 30). Consequently the primary approach available to the Dutch has been to cultivate working relationships with these newer immigrant denominations across denominational lines. By contrast, more than 150 of the CRC's 1,000 congregations are made up primarily of persons of color. Another difference is that the Dutch study focuses more on community development, ecumenism, and partnership issues, whereas the CRC has worked harder at evangelizing, church planting, and racial reconciliation.

A third difference relates to the status and nature of immigrant churches. In countries such as the Netherlands, the historic or mainline Reformed churches are indigenous to the countries in which they were founded; virtually all immigrants are relative newcomers and are persons of color. By contrast, North American denominations with European roots may be considered mainline churches, but at the same time are historically immigrant churches as well. This certainly is true of the CRC.

In October 2003, Borgdorff and Mulder interviewed Dr. Sjaak van't Kruis, who wrote *Born in Zion* (2001), and Ms. Elza Kuyk, lead contributor to *Relations with Migrant Churches* (2002).

9

A related dimension is our differing histories regarding the concept of race. Even though Europeans introduced the "race" construct as a distinguishing feature of people groups worldwide, "race" became a defining and organizing principle in North America in ways that Europeans had neither intended nor imagined. (See origin and meaning of race, pp. 11-12, and an overview of our "racialized" United States and Canadian culture, chapter 1.)

WHAT LANGUAGE SHALL WE BORROW?

Speaking of "mainline" and "immigrant" churches may be accurate in certain European or international settings, but the North American context requires different terminology. For the CRC specifically, the early focus is the "Dutch immigrant" character of the CRC in relation to a variety of racial and ethnic stories.

In 1995, a Calvin College social research project reported that 89 percent of all members in the CRC claimed full or partial Dutch ancestry.

Many of these "other" people groups that are now part of the CRC are immigrants—for the most part, Asian Americans and Latin Americans. However, the distinguishing history of most persons of African descent, particularly in the United States, is not one of immigration but of enslavement and oppression. Similarly, First Nations people in Canada and Native Americans in the United States—while having migrated here once upon a time—certainly are not immigrants. These multiple story lines are all wrapped into the title *Learning to Count to One: The Joy and Pain of Becoming a Multiracial Church.* To help us in our thinking and conversation, we need to clarify some of the reoccurring terminology used in this study.

MULTIETHNIC

Churches with people from various races and countries of origin are often described as *multi-ethnic.* The word *ethnic* comes from the Greek word *ethnee* and refers to nations or people groups. (A biblical example is the people groups named on Pentecost Sunday: "Parthians, Medes and Elamites; residents of Mesopotamia, Judea and Cappadocia, Pontus and Asia. . . ." Acts 2:9).

Too frequently *ethnic* is used as a code word for *race*—referring specifically to people who are *not white,* or as a synonym for population groups whose first language is not English.

Strictly speaking, *ethnicity* refers to one's country of origin. In this sense, perhaps, most white gatherings in North America today are multiethnic. Hispanic leaders are quick to point out that many Hispanic congregations in North America also include multiple ethnicities: persons from Argentina, Costa Rica, Cuba, Mexico, Nicaragua, Puerto Rico, Peru, and more. The point is that a *multiethnic* congregation, while a beautiful creation of God, is not necessarily multiracial.

Since the 1970s the CRC has tended to use *ethnic* as a catch-all term that includes indigenous peoples in Canada and the United States, all persons of African descent, Hispanics of whatever hue, and all other non-white immigrants in Canada and the U.S.

Multicultural

For the sociologist, culture includes such factors as age, economic status, educational levels, gender, geography, language, national origin, political preference, sexual orientation, race, religion, and more. According to the dictionary, culture has a whole range of meanings from artistic and intellectual pursuits to the sum total of how a nation thinks and acts—for example, the Greek culture.

So from one perspective, the term *multicultural* is too generic. When you consider the inclusiveness of culture—economics, education, behavior, age differences—every congregation is multicultural, *with or without* ethnic and racial diversity. From another perspective, however, *multicultural* is comprehensive, including core identity and default behavior plus skin color and national origin. God's grand new community, drawn from "every tribe and language and people and nation" (Rev. 5:9), is perhaps best captured by the term *multicultural.*

Multiracial

Multiracial is another term used to describe congregations with ethnic and racial diversity. Interestingly, "*race* is actually a categorization invented a few hundred years ago by the earliest

European anthropologists to account for the human diversity that was coming to their awareness during the fifteenth and sixteenth centuries. Yet that notion of 'race,' or human subspecies, quickly revealed itself—even to fledgling anthropology— to be without scientific validity" (*The Banner,* Sept. 2004, pp. 42-43). Similarly, the Alpen Institute contends, "Scientific studies conclude that race has no biological meaning or significance. The gene for skin color is linked with no other human trait. The genes that account for intelligence, athletic ability, personality type, and even hair and eye color are independent of the gene for skin color" *(Structural Racism and Community Building,* June 2004, p. 8). How insidious that this flimsy construct—gradation in skin color—has greater social and political significance than either ethnicity or culture. Ironically, in spite of its superficial basis, division over race tends to be deeper and wider than either culture or ethnicity. In some ways, therefore, becoming *multiracial* is the greater challenge.

My general preference for the purposes of this study is to use the term *multiracial.* Recognizing, however, that no terminology is best for every situation, at times we will use the terms *multicultural* and *multiethnic* interchangeably or in combination with the term *multiracial.*

Ethnicity and Race

When possible we will identify people in relation to their national origin: Korean, Puerto Rican, Vietnamese, and so on. Some of the time, however, the context may require specific ethnic and racial categories. Although indigenous people in Canada are commonly referred to as aboriginal or First Nations, and as Native American in the U.S., generally they all prefer to be referred to by their tribal name, such as Apache or Cherokee, Navajo, or Haida. Ethnic Haitians, Jamaicans, African immigrants, African Americans, and African Canadians also, at times, refer to their shared racialized identity by the more inclusive term *black.* Other broad categories, such as Asian or Hispanic, also may

During a 1980s interview for a ministry position with the CRC, Rev. Gina Jacobs, a member of the Sioux nation and a seminary graduate, said, "I've always felt more discriminated against as an Indian than as a woman."

be useful in referring specifically to other racialized groups.

Ethnic Minority

Although this language is commonly used to describe persons who are not white, there is increasing discomfort with it. For one thing, *ethnee* is a Greek word that means a nation or people. In other words, we are all *ethnee* or ethnic. Further, whether or not we are members of an ethnic minority depends at least in part on the context. A person who is Chinese American is part of a numerical majority in Chinatown but a member of an ethnic numerical minority in the voting booth or the bank. A white pastor may be a member of an ethnic numerical minority in a black or Navajo community, but still be part of the white majority in terms of privilege and power in the broader society. Given prevailing North American practices regarding ethnicity and race, *minority* conveys lack of access or status and therefore may be a put-down. Similarly, *majority* communicates the not so subtly implied right to rule. Handle with care!

Persons of Color and White Persons

Given our "racialized" society, occasionally we need vocabulary that distinguishes between the "numerical majority" and "numerical minorities" as a whole. Although no race-based language is without difficulty, ordinarily we will use the term *white persons* for Anglos, Caucasians, and "non-Hispanic whites." And, with apologies to all, we will use the phrase "persons of color" when needing to

The billboard in front of this CRC ministry in Arcadia, California, lists separate congregational worship services in five languages: English, Chinese, Korean, Indonesian, and Spanish.

differentiate ethnic, racial, national, and cultural people groups who are not identified as white.

FROM WHOM AND TO WHOM?

Learning to Count to One is an authentic team effort. I express my appreciation to Peter Borgdorff for envisioning the project and to Patricia Nederveld for leading the publishing process. Special thanks to a committed group of writers—Harry Boonstra, Louis Tamminga, Reginald Smith, Manny Bersach, Edward Yoon, Lois and Mike Vander Pol, and John VanTil—for their chapter contributions. I praise God for those dozens of beautiful saints—persons of color and white persons—whose love for the Lord and his church prompted them to share their stories of joy and pain. Thanks to Stanley Jim, Tong Park, Robert Price, and Gary Teja for their helpful advice in the concept stage of the project. Thanks also to Viviana Cornejo for timely assistance with chapter 6, and to Art Hoekstra for his expert screening out of race bias in our language. Finally, I was encouraged and supported by the journalistic eyes and mission heart of my daughter Bonny Mulder-Behnia, and her material contribution to chapter 10. Whether you are a congregational leader or conscientious disciple, *Learning to Count to One* will inform and challenge you regarding God's vision for the church in our North American context. If you are looking for small group or adult education materials, I pray that these stories will help you reflect together on your world and life witness as twenty-first century followers of Jesus. In his letter to the diverse congregation in ancient Rome, the apostle Paul emphatically reminded these early Christians, *"So in Christ we who are many form one body, and each member belongs to all the others"* (12:5). The angel who spoke to the seven churches in Asia Minor a generation later says to us as well: "Anyone who is willing to hear should listen to the Spirit and understand what the Spirit is saying to the churches" (Rev. 2:7a, New Living Translation).

—Al Mulder
September 2005

CHAPTER ONE

DISCOVERING A CONTINENT
Alfred E. Mulder

"... from every tribe and language and people and nation ...." —Revelation 5:9

We met at the city library. I was looking for resource materials, and she offered her assistance. It took us a while. The very next Sunday, as I was leaving our early service, I met her again as she was walking up for the second service. We were surprised to realize we attended the same congregation. We greeted each other cordially and introduced ourselves again. We asked about each other's faith walk and families. When she asked about my work, I told her I was a minister and that I helped the Christian Reformed Church start new Christian Reformed congregations. She then said to me in utter amazement, "Why would anyone want to start another Christian Reformed Church?"

She was enthusiastic about our own congregation, but believed that "we" were different from the rest of the CRC. Living among a concentration of CRC congregations in western Michigan, she had a very negative view of the CRC as a whole.

WHAT DID THE CRC FIRST LOOK LIKE?

In the 1840s hundreds of Dutch-speaking folks immigrated to the United States and located in West Michigan. Many of them came as congregations—with a pastor, elders, and deacons already in place. By 1849, seven West Michigan immigrant congregations—nearly 1,000 persons strong—had organized themselves as "Classis Holland." In 1850, with the coaxing of Rev. Wyckoff from New York, they affiliated with the United States-based counterpart of the Netherlands state church, the Dutch Reformed Church (now the Reformed Church in America).

Before long, complaints began circulating among the new immigrant churches: too many hymns were being sung, the Lord's Supper was open to Christians of non-Reformed traditions, catechism instruction was being neglected, and "what grieves our hearts most in all of this is that there are members among you who regard our secession in the Netherlands as not strictly necessary, or that it was untimely." Besides, some argued, Rev. Wyckoff "gives us liberty to walk in this ecclesiastical path." (*Torch and Trumpet*, April 1957).

According to T. Ulberg, the Vriesland group also complained that "colored communicants were seated apart from the rest at the table of the Lord." This complaint was not repeated as a ground for seceding from its older sister denomination.

So after a tentative seven-year relationship, five immigrant congregations with two ministers and 750 members separated from the RCA. With one minister serving as president and the other as clerk, they held an organizational meeting on April 29, 1857. And that is how the Christian Reformed Church was born. (One congregation and one minister, Rev. Klijn, returned to the Dutch Reformed Church during the first year.)

Immigrants do not arrive without baggage. Hardly a generation earlier, many of these same folks had objected to similar practices in the state-sanctioned Reformed Church in the Netherlands. Their protests had little effect, and in 1834 a number of Dutch congregations officially separated or *seceded* from their mother church. The Dutch government held a dim view of secession, and the seceders suffered significant personal loss (more about this in chapter 2). Understandably, they were skittish about being linked with anyone who might not be totally like-minded.

This is not to say that the seceders made their complaints flippantly. They were tough-minded people with courage and conviction who put their lives on the line for what they believed. They valued the

Reformed tradition and championed orthodoxy as they understood it. How could they "trust" a denomination, historically Dutch and Reformed or otherwise, that failed to appreciate the recent struggles in their homeland? Thus, separated from their motherland by the Atlantic Ocean and from their new homeland by language and culture, this small but determined band of seceders further isolated themselves by going it on their own—again.

IN WHAT GARDEN DID WE GROW?

As a boy attending a one-room Iowa country school in the 1940s, I was impressed with the magnanimous spirit of the Declaration of Independence by the United States of America: "We hold these truths to be self-evident, that all men are created equal, that they are endowed by their Creator with certain unalienable Rights, that among these are Life, Liberty, and the pursuit of Happiness. . . . That whenever any Form of Government becomes destructive of these ends, it is the Right of the People to alter or to abolish it and to institute new Government . . . in such form as to them shall seem most likely to effect their Safety and Happiness."

As a man starting ministry in the 1960s, I gradually became aware that this magnanimous spirit applied readily to white America—but only reluctantly to other Americans. Ironically, this language allowed a prevailing view—among whites at least—that white persons were created superior to other persons. In spite of these glorious words, many still believed that men were created more equal than women, and that white citizens were guaranteed more "unalienable Rights" than others.

I gradually realized how inconsistently we as Christians truly rise above the culture of which we are a part. I say this about my sometimes complicit role in missionary work among Navajos and Zunis in the Southwest—from boarding schools patterned after the United States government to our paternalistic approach

One of two ministers in the CRC, and for a time the only one, the Rev. Koene Vanden Bosch had newly emigrated from the Netherlands. The Noordeloos CRC centennial booklet described their first pastor this way: "Rev. Vanden Bosch was a man of staunch religious convictions and found it extremely difficult to accept convictions other than his own. For him to forgive someone who had wronged him did not come easily."

In the mid-1900s, one-room country schools dotted the Iowa countryside—often one every four square miles. The author attended Center Township #5 through grade 7, at which time his parents transferred him to the Christian school in Ireton, Iowa.

in training native leaders. I say this about our general difficulty in distinguishing between religious truth and religious tradition, and between Christian convictions and cultural conditioning.

This is why it is so important to understand the context in which we were birthed and grew. We need to reexamine our national histories and how they bear on our personal attitudes and corporate identity—especially in relation to race and culture.

FINDERS, KEEPERS?

The early development and colonization of Canada and the United States was a natural outgrowth of prevailing attitudes among Christians toward the un-Christianized world. The Roman papacy and European monarchs alike touted the belief, also called the Doctrine of Discovery, that the "heathen" were unworthy to possess the physical wealth of God's creation. In 1482 King Henry VII of England said it this way: "Seek out, discover, and find what so ever islands, countries, regions, or provinces of the heathens and infidels, what so ever they be, and in what part of the world so ever they be, which before this time have been unknown to Christians" (Haudenasaunee UN Intervention, and Sardar and Davies, p. 144). Christian nations were encouraged to "discover" land occupied by non-Christian people and claim it for advancing God's purposes. Ten years later Columbus "discovered" America, and five years after that Cabot "discovered" Canada. The idea was simple: finders, keepers!

Finding Land

Obviously this philosophy was custom-made for North American settlers in securing land then occupied by "heathen" natives. For the vast majority of our shared histories, our two nations "discovered" both used and unused lands—from sea to shining sea. Sometimes the newcomers paid reasonable prices, and sometimes absurd prices. Far too often they simply took land because they could. For centuries, aboriginal peoples in

Canada and Native Americans in the Unites States were denied the right to vote or hold property. Both countries adopted Reservation Acts. Both countries reduced the lands available for native use, expanding the resources available to newcomers. Both countries developed and operated boarding schools that separated Indian children from their parents in order to "civilize" them.

The heart of the strategy was devaluing Native people as inferior or less than human—as "wild savages." Commenting on the adage that "The only good Indian is a dead Indian," future present Theodore Roosevelt said in 1886, "I don't go so far as to think that the only good Indians are dead Indians, but I believe nine out of every ten are, and I shouldn't like to inquire too closely into the tenth. The most vicious cowboy has more moral principle than the average Indian." In 1895 some synodical delegates argued against sending missionaries among Native Americans "since Indians are a dying race." The net result of such attitudes has been incredible devastation and degradation of Native populations in the United States and Canada in the name of civilization and progress. Four hundred years after being "discovered," the majority of First Nations people scratch out a marginalized existence on government reserves, while the heirs of Europeans hold title to the majority of the land and resources.

Both countries developed and operated boarding schools that separated Indian children from their parents in order to "civilize" them.

Finding Labor

Another major factor in the early development of our nations, particularly the United States, was the practice of enslavement. The ancestors of the overwhelming majority of African Americans today were brought to North America for enslavement during the 1600s and 1700s. Driven by the desire for cheap labor, the slave trade flourished in the southern British colonies. Slavery also was accepted in the Spanish colony of Florida, the French colony of Louisiana, and to a degree in New France (now Quebec) and British Canada.

To some extent the prevailing attitude toward enslavement swung back and forth. Prior to New Netherland (now New York) becoming a British colony in 1664, English courts generally had held that when enslaved people from Africa became Christians, they were to be set free. In 1665 Dutch governor Peter Stuyvesant did the British one better by also defending the right of free blacks to own land. However, between then and 1704, six colonies, including New York and New Jersey, passed legislation making it legal for Christians to remain enslaved. Virginia went one step further, declaring that if a master were to kill an enslaved person in the course of giving correction, the master *"shall be free and acquitted of all punishment and accusation for the same, as if such accident had never happened"* (Virginia Colony Slave Codes, Article 34). In 1712 the New York Assembly passed a law forcing free blacks to sell their lands (including the land upon which the Empire State Building stands).

Within the Reformed tradition, attitudes were similar to those in broader society. In 1747 Classis Amsterdam of the RCA still was of a mind that becoming a Christian did not entitle an enslaved person to be set free. In 1812 the general synod of the RCA affirmed that "in the church there is no difference between bond and free, but all are one in Christ," adding that blacks are to enjoy the same privileges as other members and are to be enumerated along with other members. It did not, however, condemn the practice of enslavement.

How Does a Nation Define Itself?

For nearly three hundred years, the colonies in Canada and the United States were dependent on the European powers that had "discovered" them or won them as pawns of war. During the so-called French and Indian War—more accurately, French-and-Indians-against-the-British War—first Quebec fell to the British; and by 1763 France surrendered all its territory east of the Mississippi to British rule.

Citizenship

For the next 186 years, Canadians accepted being defined as "British subjects." The American colonies, however, were not so inclined. In 1776, after only thirteen years under British rule, the colonial leaders signed the Declaration of Independence, thereby sparking the Revolutionary War against Britain. Not so incidentally, with significant assistance from both the French and the Indians, the colonists prevailed.

In 1790, as one of the functions of a newly sovereign nation, the U.S. Congress ruled that naturalized citizenship would be reserved for *"any alien, being a free white person"* (U.S. Naturalization Law of 1790). Native Americans, of course, were not alien, African Americans were not free, and neither group was white. The patterns of earlier times had created the mold for the future. The attitudes of earlier times were now baked into law. Thus began a legalized system of U.S. apartheid.

Enslavement

Enslavement was never a prominent theme in Canada, but it is part of the story. The largest slave "transaction" took place in 1783 when British Loyalists brought two thousand slaves from Africa and distributed them in three Canadian territories. Ten years later, in 1793, the Legislature of Upper Canada (now Ontario) outlawed the importation of new slaves to their colony. Then, in 1834, the British Parliament condemned both the importation and the practice of enslavement throughout the British Empire—including Canada.

Millions of citizens and immigrants alike were moving west and clamoring for land. The U.S. vision to extend its "boundaries of freedom" collided with the interests of Mexico, sparking war with Mexico in 1845. The final score: in exchange for fifteen million dollars in damages, the U.S. "annexed" what is now Arizona, California, New Mexico, Texas, and parts of Colorado, Nevada, and Utah. The treaty was signed at Guadalupe Hidalgo in 1848, the same year that Van Raalte and his band of Dutch immigrants began sinking their roots into West Michigan soil.

From the 1830s to the 1860s the practice of enslavement connected the two countries in a clandestine way. From the time the British Parliament outlawed enslavement among its subjects to the time the United States abolished enslavement by going to war against itself, tens of thousands of African Americans fled enslavement by crossing to Canada with the help of the Underground Railroad.

The story of the United States is painfully different! Although the United States actually prohibited the *importation* of slaves in 1807, the practice of enslavement survived and thrived in the southern states until it was put to death by the American Civil War. The war began in 1861 (four years after the birth of the CRC). President Abraham Lincoln issued the Emancipation Proclamation in 1863. Two years later, enslavement was finally and officially outlawed by the Thirteenth Amendment to the Constitution of the United States. In 1868 the Fourteenth Amendment granted full U.S. citizenship to African Americans, and in 1870 the Fifteenth Amendment gave black males the right to vote.

Inequality

As clear-cut as these actions seem, race prejudice and white dominance persisted. Initially, southern blacks made great strides toward equal rights. But as soon as Union troops were withdrawn, southern states quickly enacted laws to limit blacks' access to transportation, schools, restaurants, and other public facilities. The Ku Klux Klan used cross burnings and other forms of violence and intimidation to perpetuate white supremacy. Thousands of black men and women were openly lynched. Most southern blacks continued to live in grinding poverty.

Race wars continued on other fronts as well.

- "In 1868 General Grant, who continued as Commanding General of the Army after the Civil War and before his presidency, insisted that he would protect the westward movement of white settlers 'even if the extermination of every Indian tribe was necessary to secure such a result'"(*Native American Voices*, p. 85).

- That same year the Navajos were corralled like animals and marched across New Mexico to confinement in Fort Sumner.

- In 1879 the U.S. government sponsored its first boarding school for Indian youngsters, and by 1886 was appealing to the churches to take a more active role in this "civilizing" process.

- In 1882 Congress approved the Chinese Exclusion Act, specifically prohibiting the naturalization of Chinese persons as citizens.

- In 1896 the U.S. Supreme Court upheld the "separate but equal" doctrine—thereby continuing "colored sections" in public places. Nineteenth-century Canada paralleled its southern neighbor.

- In the 1850s British Columbia allowed the segregation of African Canadians in its public schools.

- In 1870 aboriginal people and people of Chinese and Japanese descent were denied the right to vote.

- That same decade saw the approval of the Indian Act, which expanded aboriginal "reserves" and restricted aboriginal rights and cultural practices.

- Beginning in the 1890s, aboriginal children were sent away to residential schools—opening the door to abuses that haunt the Canadian government, sponsoring churches, and, of course, the First Nations people more than a century later.

HOW LONG, O LORD, HOW LONG?

In the first half of the twentieth century, the U.S. remained busy managing the contradiction between its declaration of "liberty and justice for all" and its practice of discrimination and injustice toward persons of color—while delivering

Reaching Out, 1889-1949

1889—Missionary to the Sioux in South Dakota, left after one year

1896—Missionary couples to the Navajo in Arizona/New Mexico

1897—One of the couples relocates to Zuni, New Mexico

1903—Founding of the "Mission" in Rehoboth, New Mexico

1905—First CRC organized in Canada: Nijverdal CRC, near Monarch, Alberta (the Granum and Nobleford CRCs both trace their roots to the Nijverdal congregation)

1907—First CRC missionary to Dutch immigrants in Canada

1918—Mission to the Jews: Chicago and Eastern U.S.

1920—First secretary/director installed for Foreign and Indian Missions

1922—First missionary couples sent to China, workers expelled 1942

1923—Johanna Veenstra begins work in Nigeria "on her own"

1930—First missionaries to Argentina

1939—The CRC began radio broadcasting in English

1940—CRC officially approves missionary work in Nigeria

1947—First secretary/director installed for Home Missions work

1949—Start of mission work in Ceylon

race-based power and privilege to people who could qualify as white. Puerto Rico and the Philippines had become U.S. possessions by way of the Spanish-American War. A 1917 Immigration Act introduced the "Asiatic Barred Zone," preventing immigration from both Asia and India. The Supreme Court denied appeals for citizenship by a Japanese American and an Asian-Indian American, grounded in the court's own race-based views of whiteness. Simultaneously, Congress granted citizenship to "all non-citizen (American) Indians born within the territorial limits of the United States." The traumatic years of World War II were marked by two contrasting developments: the superb contribution of the "Navajo code talkers" in the war against Japan, and the shameful confinement of American residents of Japanese origin.

Midway through the twentieth century, the U.S. finally began facing down its phobia over race. In 1954 the U.S. Supreme Court—in the case of Brown *v.* the Board of Education—made its historic unanimous ruling that "separate educational facilities are inherently unequal." This ruling helped fuel the U.S. Civil Rights Movement. Blacks boycotted segregated public transportation in southern states. Civil rights groups organized voter registration campaigns, Freedom Rides, and other protest actions. White segregationists fought back with intimidation and violence, and southern law enforcement used cattle prods and attack dogs, fire hoses and mass arrests. An emotional high point in the movement was the massive 1963 March on Washington for Jobs and Freedom, and Martin Luther King's "I Have a Dream" speech on the steps of the Lincoln Memorial. A legislative high point was the congressional approval of the Civil Rights Acts of 1964, banning discrimination in public accommodations, employment, and labor unions. This legal centerpiece was fortified by the Voting Rights Act of 1965 and the American Indian Civil Rights Act of 1968.

In a similar time frame, Canada created its own version of a more welcoming nation. The Citizenship Act of 1947 was key to reshaping Canadian identity from European Canadian subjects of the British throne to a distinctly Canadian vision of a multicultural society. In 1960 Canada adopted a Bill of Rights, rejecting discrimination based on such considerations as race, national origin, religion or gender, and in 1964 prohibited any further segregation of black Canadians in its public schools. The Citizenship Act of 1977 made Canadian citizenship more accessible by reducing prior conditions for immigrants and by eliminating discrimination on the basis of nationality and gender.

Dr. Martin Luther King, Jr. and Mrs. King marching to Montgomery, Alabama, 1965

Finally, four and a half centuries after Columbus and Cabot set foot on North American soil, "all" legally came to mean "all." (*Author's note:* This overview is informed significantly by the research and analysis of Crossroads Ministries and its co-executive director Robette Diaz, and by CRC Campus Pastor Shiao Chong of Toronto, Ontario.)

HOW DOES A CHURCH DEFINE ITSELF?

As we reflect on attitudes and actions regarding ethnicity and race in our North American context, I would love to compare the CRC to the "men of Issachar, who understood the times and knew what [the people of God] should do" (1 Chron. 12:32). The reality is that sometimes we led, sometimes we followed, and sometimes we were in the way. Whether our ancestors arrived in North America in 800 or 1600 or 2000, we've all been racialized. The same is true of Christian organizations. Even in the church, we still share privilege and power unevenly. Persons in a numerical racial minority are not always truly welcome and frequently are at risk. Similarly, persons in the racial majority often are affirmed and empowered on the basis of their identity with the majority race, not on their identity in Christ. Our attitudes and actions as Christians are infected by the culture around us as surely as by the promptings of the Spirit and Word within us.

A genuine "race crisis" erupted in the CRC in the late 1960s, when children of black families from the Lawndale CRC in Chicago were denied admission to Timothy Christian School in Cicero. Synod 1968 faced the crisis head-on. It declared a day of prayer and called all members to "give themselves to repentance and to public and private prayer." It affirmed that those who persisted in racial discrimination would be subject to church

photo by Duane E. Vander Brug

Lawndale children at Des Plaines Christian School

discipline. And it mandated its board of Home Missions "to design, organize and implement programs . . . to eliminate racism, both causes and effect, within the body of believers and throughout the world in which we live" (*Acts of Synod* 1968).

In 1971 synod transferred this mandate to a new standing Race Relations committee made up of people from various racial backgrounds and reporting directly to synod. Race Relations, first directed by white persons but subsequently by CRC persons of color, implemented a wide range of strategies for improving understanding and racial reconciliation. These strategies still include celebrating an annual National Heritage Sunday and sponsoring a biennial church-wide Multiethnic Conference. In its early years Race Relations also involved itself in the struggle against the system of apartheid in South Africa, and cautioned—at home—that "in her pastoral ministry the church should strive to eradicate attitudes of racial superiority . . ." (*Acts of Synod* 1979).

In recent decades the CRC has enjoyed increasing racial and ethnic diversity. One contributing factor was the acceleration of planting new congregations, increasing from an average of five per year in the 1970s to ten per year in the 80s, and twenty per year in the 90s. Remarkably, of the last three hundred new church starts in the CRC, more than half were among immigrant communities or racially diverse populations. In twenty-five years CRC Korean congregations mushroomed to ninety strong, Hispanic congregations more than doubled, and Southeast Asian groups bubbled up across the continent. And more congregations—initially all white or all persons of color—are praying hard and working hard to become multicultural.

Increased church planting was complemented by welcoming actions at other levels. Synod relaxed its rules for receiving ministers from other denominations, declaring that "for multicultural or ethnic minority churches the need for indigenous leadership shall constitute the criterion for meeting the 'need' requirements of . . . the Church Order" (Synod 1985, Church Order Articles 7, 8). Also, a growing number of classes embraced substantial racial diversity—from a "minority majority" in Red Mesa and Pacific Hanmi to a deepening mosaic in classes such as California South, Greater Los Angeles, Hackensack, and Southwest U.S.

Reaching Across, 1951-1979

1950—Rev. Eugene Callendar began work among African Americans in Harlem, New York

1951—Rev. Paul Szto began work among Chinese immigrants in Queens, New York

1956—First all-Navajo congregation organized: Bethany CRC, Gallup, New Mexico

1960—"Off-reservation" Indian work transferred from World Missions to Home Missions

1962—Rev. Scott Redhouse became first Navajo to be ordained as CRC minister

1964—"Reservation" Indian work transferred from World Missions to Home Missions

1964—First Spanish-language congregation organized in Miami, Florida

1974—CRC ministry to Canadian aboriginal peoples began in Winnipeg, Manitoba

1977—First CRC Korean congregation of Los Angeles organized, left in 1994

1979—First church planting ministry among Chinese Canadians Abbotsford (Zion) and Richmond, British Columbia

In Reformed church polity, an officially connected cluster of congregations is a *classis* (plural, *classes*). Classis is the middle assembly between local councils and the general synod.

What Does the CRC Look Like Today?

At Pentecost the Holy Spirit was given to the church. In pouring out the Spirit on many peoples, God overcomes the divisions of Babel; now people from every tongue, tribe, and nation are gathered into the unity of the body of Christ.

From a handful of isolationist Dutch immigrant congregations, God has been graciously growing the CRC as an increasingly diverse family of nearly one thousand congregations. They are distributed throughout nine provinces and thirty-nine states—plus Guam, Puerto Rico, and Washington, D.C. Although still very predominantly white and of Dutch ancestry, the family circle includes Native Americans and African Americans. It contains Canadian aboriginal peoples, Quebecois, and new African immigrants. It embraces persons of Cambodian, Chinese, Indonesian, Filipino, Korean, Laotian, Pakistani, and Vietnamese descent. It is further enriched with persons of Latin origin from more than a dozen Spanish-speaking countries.

How God is overcoming the divisions of Babel is what the rest of this book is all about.

DISCUSSION STARTERS

1. Read and reflect on Isaiah 60:1-3, "The Glory of Zion." What do these verses suggest about God's plan for his church?

2. What is the relationship between truth and love? Which is more important? Evaluate in relation to the attitudes of our "CRC founding fathers" and prevailing attitudes among Christians today.

3. Miroslav Volf wrote, "Our coziness with the culture has made us so blind to many of its evils." Are we also blind to evil in the culture of others, or only in our own? Why?

4. Compare the earliest U.S. definition of citizenship to Paul's definition of citizenship in Philippians 3:18-21.

5. In a predominantly white residential area of Grand Rapids, Michigan, a public elementary school is 95 percent black and Hispanic. Right across the street a Christian school is 95 percent white. How might that picture be "inherently unequal"?

6. In 1903 black intellectual W.E.B. Du Bois introduced his now classic treatise *The Soul of Black Folks* by saying that "the problem of the twentieth century is the problem of the color line." In what ways is "the problem of the color line" unfinished business for churches in North America in the twenty-first century?

CHRONOLOGY OF RACE

>>>Late 1400s and ff. >>>

United States

1492	1540	1628	1642	1664
Columbus "discovers" America under flag of Spain	Spaniards came to SW Hopi and Zuni pueblos	Slaves arrived in New Amsterdam, freed slaves owned land in 1644	Gov. Kieft of New Amsterdam led soldiers in murderous raid on Algonquins	British seized New Netherland and renamed it New York

Pre-CRC History

1481	1517	1536	1561	1618-1619	1628	1663
King Henry VII of Britain affirmed Christian "Doctrine of Discovery"	Martin Luther nailed 95 theses on church door	John Calvin's *Institutes of the Christian Religion*	Belgic Confession 1563 Heidelberg Catechism	Synod of Dort, Canons of Dort	First Dutch Reformed congregation in New Netherland (New York)	John Eliot translated the Bible into the Algonquin language

Canada

1497	1534	1628	1600s	1639
John Cabot of England arrived on east coast of Canada	Jacques Cartier raised French flag on Gaspé Peninsula	First black resident of Canada (New France/ Quebec) was a slave	French policy encouraged intermarriage with aboriginal peoples to create one new people	Usuline Catholics established convent schools to prepare aboriginal girls to marry Christian men

>>>Late 1600s and ff. >>>

United States

1756-1763	1763	1776	1789	1790
French and Indian War—resistance to British	France ceded all territory east of the Mississippi to British rule; Louisiana to Spain	Colonies declared their independence against British rule	New Constitution takes effect; Indian Affairs assigned to the War Department	Naturalization Law granted US citizenship to "any alien being a free white person"

Pre-CRC History

1690	1740s	1747	1774	1779
Indian converts received into Reformed Church in Albany, NY	Great Awakening in American colonies	Classis New Amsterdam of RCA ruled that converted slaves were not free.	Pennsylvania Quakers disowned slaveholding members	John Newton, former slave ship captain, wrote "Amazing Grace"

Canada

1689	1709	1759	1763	1774	1783	1780s
King Louis XIV of France authorized slavery in Canada	Assembly of Lower Canada confirmed legality of slavery	New France (Quebec) was brought under British rule	Proclamation that lands cannot be taken from aboriginal peoples without a treaty	Quebec Act restored and expanded some of its borders	British Loyalists brought 2,000 African slaves to British Canada	Nova Scotia's administration encroaches on Micmac land without treaty

United States

1793	1812	1812 ff.	1830-1939	1845-1848	1848	1861-1863	1863
US Abolition Act and start of Underground Railroad to Canada	Following War of 1812, the US-Canadian border remained open	Over 2,000 US blacks migrated to Canada after the war	President Jackson's Indian Removal Act and "The Trail of Tears"	War with Mexico; US annexed vast land areas in the Southwest	US Federal (Indian) Reservation Act	Beginning of US Civil War; Lincoln issued Emancipation Proclamation	Navajo people began "long walk" to Fort Sumner, NM, enforced by the US Army

Pre-CRC and CRC History

1816	1820s-1840s	1834	1848	1857
Reformed Church in America counted blacks as members	Methodists and Anglicans started residential schools in Canada	Concerned congregations in Netherlands "seceded" from Dutch state church	Van Raalte and wave of Dutch immigrants relocated in West Michigan	Several Dutch immigrant "seceder" congregations began CRC in W. Michigan

Canada

1807	1812	1815	1834	1830-1860s	1850s	1867
Canada congress ends importation of kidnapped and enslaved Africans	Canadian and British troops repulsed an attempted US invasion	Nova Scotia passes resolution that no more black people can settle in the province	British Parliament abolished slavery in the British empire	Many thousands of African American slaves fled to Canada; 75% returned after US Civil War	Ontario allowed segregation of African Canadians in their schools	Canada became a Federation with its first prime minister

>>>1860s and ff .>>>

United States

1868	1979	1882	1890	1890		1917	1924
US makes treaty with the Navajo people, "released" to return home on foot	First boarding school for Indian youth on military training base Carlisle, PA	Chinese Exclusion Act, prohibiting immigration of Chinese	Massacre at Wounded Knee in South Dakota	US Supreme Court upheld the "separate but equal" doctrine		Immigration Act, which included the "Asiatic Barred Zone"	Native Americans granted full US citizenship

CRC History

1876	1885	1888		1896		1918	1922
CRC installs Geert Boer as its first full-time professor of theology	Secessionist branch in the Netherlands encouraged immigrants to join the CRC	CRC sent missionary to the Sioux; he left after one year		CRC sent missionary couples to the Navajo and Zuni people		Mission to Jews on East Coast and in Chicago	Missionaries were sent to China; Johanna Veenstra went to Africa in 1923

Canada

1870s	1876	1884	1890s		1907	1908	
Aboriginal peoples, Chinese, and Japanese denied right to vote	Indian Act expanded aboriginal reserves, other rules	Various aboriginal practices banned, (bans lifted 1951)	Aboriginal children sent away to residential schools		Asiatic Exclusion League led riot against Chinese and Japanese in Vancouver	BC schools were allowed to exclude students on racial grounds	

United States

1944	1954	1964	1965-68	1990
Navajo Code Talkers help win WW II	Supreme Court makes landmark decision that "separate is not equal"	Civil Rights Act banned discrimination in schools and other public arenas	Voting Rights Act & American Indian Civil Rights Act	Prohibiting use of native languages in schools repealed by president

CRC History

1940	1956	1968	1970	1983	1995	1996
Missionaries officially sent to Nigeria	First Navajo (and non-white) congregation organized in Gallup, NM	Black youth refused admission to Timothy Christian School, Chicago	Synod established committee on Race Relations	Annual All Nations Heritage Sunday initiated	Synod appoints ethnic advisors to synod	Study report on "Diverse and Unified Family of God"

Canada

1945	1947	1960	1960s	1974	1982	1988	1998
University of Manitoba dropped admission quotas for "non-preferred' groups	Canada established citizenship with new multicultural identity	Bill of Rights rejected discrimination on the basis of race, national origin, gender, and religion	Aboriginal persons granted the right to vote	Canadian CRC began work among First Nations people in Winnipeg	Canada Act brings "home" the Canadian Constitution including the Charter of Rights and Freedoms	Last residential school in Canada closed	Government apologized to indigenous people for 150 years of mistreatment

1999

CRC
agencies &
institutions
began
antiracism
training
and
organizing

CHAPTER TWO

THE CHRISTIAN REFORMED CHURCH: ITS IMMIGRANT ROOTS

Harry Boonstra

"How shall we sing the Lord's song in a foreign land?" —Psalm 137:4, RSV

Who were these Christian Reformed folks who stuck together so tightly in their Dutch immigrant churches and communities? Why did they isolate themselves for so long from the American mainstream? Why were their churches so inept for generations at enfolding people from other races and cultures? How could they so enthusiastically embrace a biblical world-and-life view, yet be so reluctant to affirm the biblical teaching about the unity of the body of Christ?

HOW DID THE DENOMINATION BEGIN?

The Reformed Church in the Netherlands was birthed in the Protestant Reformation of the 1500s and 1600s, and virtually became a national church or government-operated church. Theological errors crept in under the influence of European "liberalism," and many ministers no longer believed or taught the essentials of the Christian faith.

Some sincere believers responded to this liberalism by forming "conventicles," small groups of people who met in homes to read illustrious Reformed writers, listen to lay preachers, testify to their own faith, and pray together. Another response was a revival among a smaller group of ministers who sought to reemphasize key Reformation teachings.

Dissatisfaction came to a head in 1834 when Rev. Hendrik de Cock and his congregation in the village of Ulrum separated from the national church, the *Hervormde Kerk*. Soon other ministers and congregations joined the Secession of 1834. The Dutch church and the Dutch government responded harshly with jail time, fines, and violence. These actions only seemed to fuel the movement, as another group separated from the national Dutch church in 1886. The two seceder groups united in 1892 as the Reformed Churches in the Netherlands. Immigrants from both of these groups had great influence in the development of the CRC.

The Ulrum church seceded from the national Dutch church in 1834.

Pastor Albertus C. Van Raalte, an 1834 seceder, and some forty followers reached Western Michigan in 1847. Today it's difficult to imagine the incredible obstacles this small band faced. They were unskilled in tree felling, short on food and funds, unaccustomed to the extremes of winter snow and summer heat, racked by illness and death, and challenged by new geography and new language. The vision of Van Raalte's utopian Christian community must have seemed a cruel chimera those first years. Yet these immigrants courageously fought through dense forests by ox cart and on foot. They felled trees, planted gardens, built sod huts and later cabins and houses, attempted to learn English, organized their congregations, and founded schools. The achievements of this first settlement in West Michigan contributed to a sense of pride and cohesion among later Dutch immigrants.

When Van Raalte first arrived in New York in 1846, he had been welcomed by a pastor from the Reformed Protestant Dutch Church, Isaac Wyckoff. This denomination, now the Reformed Church in America, had been founded in New York by Dutch settlers long before, in 1628. As Van Raalte and his growing group began sinking roots in Michigan, the Reformed Church invited the emerging immigrant churches to become part of their fellowship. In 1850 Van Raalte and company did just that, joining the Reformed Church as a separate classis—Holland.

However, this union was soon challenged. Critics among the new immigrants charged that some Reformed Church practices and teachings—such as inviting Christians from other denominations to the Lord's Supper and failing to teach the catechism—could not pass theological muster. The issue came to a head in 1857. Five congregations and two ministers separated themselves from the Reformed Church's Classis Holland (although within a year one congregation and one minister returned). The new church called itself variously the Dutch Reformed Church, the True Dutch Reformed Church (*Ware Hollandsche Gereformeerde Kerk*), and, since 1894, the Christian Reformed Church.

These few sentences do not begin to portray the struggle these immigrant Christians engaged in about theology, liturgical practices, and ownership of church buildings, nor the clash of personalities and strife among families and friends. The controversies tore apart the immigrant communities and damaged the relationship between the Reformed Church and the Christian Reformed

Church for generations. Only within the past few decades are wounds being healed. In recent years the two churches have begun cooperating at both congregational and denominational levels.

WHY THIS EXODUS FROM THE NETHERLANDS?

Deplorable economic conditions in the Netherlands at the time of Van Raalte, especially the potato blight, pushed many people toward immigration. Immigrants wrote glowing letters about America to their families and friends back in the Netherlands, and soon many more joined the early colonists in hope of a better financial future for their families. A second wave of emigration after World War II was also prompted largely by economic considerations. The war had left much of the Netherlands in shambles, and young people especially saw little hope for adequate employment.

Economics, of course, were not the only reason for emigrating. Some people emigrated because they missed their families and friends who already lived in America (as was true for my family when we emigrated to Canada in 1951). Religious considerations also were a factor, especially, as we already noted, in the early immigration of the seceders in the 1840s and 1850s. Church and government harassment of their small, struggling denomination increased the appeal of moving to the United States, where the seceders could worship in freedom and even establish Christian schools.

The immigrants themselves were as varied as the reasons that brought them. The early ministers were well educated. (Van Raalte, for example, had received his education at a *gymnasium*—a classical preparatory school—and the University of Leiden.) Many of the lay people were carpenters, tradesmen, farmers, and laborers.

The Heidelberg Catechism is a confessional statement of both the Reformed Church in America and the Christian Reformed Church. Written during the 1500s, it has been used for centuries to instruct both young and old in the teachings of the faith with a Reformed accent. In prior generations, children and young people were exposed to it in "catechism classes." The CRC Church Order also stipulates that at one of the Sunday services "the minister shall ordinarily preach the Word as summarized in the Heidelberg Catechism." The first question and answer set the tone for much of what follows:

Q. What is your only comfort in life and in death?

A. That I am not my own, but belong—body and soul, in life and in death—to my faithful Savior Jesus Christ. He has fully paid for all my sins with his precious blood, and has set me free from the tyranny of the devil. He also watches over me in such a way that not a hair can fall from my head without the will of my Father in heaven: in fact, all things must work together for my salvation. Because I belong to him, Christ, by his Holy Spirit, assures me of eternal life, and makes me wholeheartedly willing and ready from now on to live for him.

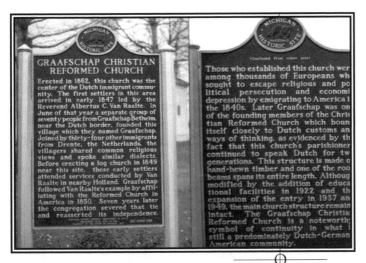

GRAAFSCHAP CHRISTIAN REFORMED CHURCH

Erected in 1862, this church was the center of the Dutch immigrant community. The first settlers in this area arrived in early 1847 led by the Reverend Albertus C. Van Raalte. In June of that year a separate group of seventy people from Graafschap Bethelm, near the Dutch border, founded this village which they named Graafschap. Joined by thirty-four other immigrants from Drente, the Netherlands, the villagers shared common religious views and spoke similar dialects. Before erecting a log church in 1849 near this site, these early settlers attended services conducted by Van Raalte in nearby Holland. Graafschap followed Van Raalte's example by affiliating with the Reformed Church in America in 1850. Seven years later the congregation severed that tie and reasserted its independence.

Those who established this church wer among thousands of Europeans wh sought to escape religious and po litical persecution and economi depression by emigrating to America i the 1840s. Later Graafschap was on of the founding members of the Chris tian Reformed Church which boun itself closely to Dutch customs an ways of thinking, as evidenced by th fact that this church's parishioner continued to speak Dutch for tw generations. This structure is made o hand-hewn timber and one of the roo beams spans its entire length. Althoug modified by the addition of educa tional facilities in 1922 and th expansion of the entry in 1937 an 1949, the main church structure remain intact. The Graafschap Christia Reformed Church is a noteworth symbol of continuity in what i still a predominately Dutch-German American community.

Graafschaap CRC, a Michigan Historic Site

The immigrants' attachment to "the old country" took different forms as well. Those who were more educated treasured the history of the Netherlands, its cultural wealth, and its Calvinist inheritance. In contrast, the common folk focused their memories on the province, village, and family they left behind. Lots of Dutch names reappeared on villages and churches in the early West Michigan "colony": Borculo, Drenthe, Graafschap, Groningen, Overisel, Vriesland, and Zeeland. Elsewhere we find several Hollands, Hollandale, Oostburg, Orange City, and South Holland—all reminiscent of the former homeland. Of course, some immigrants had no fond memories of Holland, and were happy to have escaped their own poverty and the oppressive Dutch upper class.

WHY DID THE DUTCH REMAIN DUTCH FOR SO LONG?

Certainly a potent reason for immigrants to live in tight communities is their shared culture. From Abkhazians to Zambians, immigrants tend to flock together in a new country. For some this need may last only a year; for others it may continue for generations. Nationality, traditions, customs, food, clothing, marriage, and countless other factors identify a people, and this identity can be nurtured and retained as long as they associate only with others from the same country.

For Dutch immigrants this cultural isolation also was driven by religious considerations. Van Raalte specifically *intended* that his Dutch *kolonie* would have limited dealings with American neighbors. This separation and independence, he believed, would ensure the continued religious purity of God's faithful people. Thus the Dutch ethnic community was often insular and inward, making deliberate attempts to keep the "American" world at bay. This fueled separate churches and schools and protected the marriage partner pool. In the larger communities it also resulted in the establishing of rest homes (still called Holland Homes today in several communities), sanitariums, hospitals, and funeral societies.

Along with Dutch and English, the immigrant communities created a third choice: Yankee Dutch, a curious and often humorous mixture of the two languages. For generations many people spoke both Dutch and English, either fluently or brokenly, and the circumstances often determined which. For example, folks might speak Dutch in the church council meeting, but English when selling cattle. The advertisement below shows another mixture.

An attending factor, of course, was language. Flocked together, members of these immigrant communities knew they could turn to neighbors, clerks, plumbers, newspapers, physicians, and undertakers to serve them and their needs in their own language. This unity of language was obviously most common among first generation immigrants, but it persisted as new waves of immigrants continued to arrive. For example, the Eastern Avenue congregation in Grand Rapids,

The many Dutch-language newspapers of the time also present a striking picture of the wide diffusion of language, both in articles and advertisements.

founded in 1879, recorded council minutes in Dutch until 1929. The use of the Dutch language decreased significantly during World War I, and was actually discouraged during World War II, lest "Dutch" be confused with "Deutsch," the language of the German enemy.

Education was an additional factor in encouraging community solidarity. The immigrants established a system of Christian day schools throughout the denomination, and there was strong pressure on all parents to send their children to these schools. Although this pressure has decreased greatly, as recently as twenty years ago a father likely would not have been nominated for church elder if his children did not attend the Christian school. Calvin College, the only college supported by the CRC constituency from 1908 to 1955, added to this solidarity. For many years the CRC community exerted considerable pressure on its members to attend "*onze*" (our own) Calvin College.

WHAT WAS LIFE LIKE IN A CRC COMMUNITY?

A disclaimer is in order. As I make many broad generalizations, keep in mind that we are dealing with more than one hundred years of history and hundreds of congregations. CRC customs were not always the same from one area or congregation to another, and many traditions changed over time. No doubt the most change came after the 1950s. For example, many younger people in the church today will not recognize the strict Sunday

The Faith of the Faithful

Although the isolation of Van Raalte's *kolonie* may seem inappropriately extreme, it is important to understand the context. Coming as they did from the secession church, these immigrants had fresh memories of harassment by the hierarchy of the national Dutch church. They also remembered the Dutch modernistic theology and its heresies, and were determined to maintain orthodoxy in their beliefs. Many articles and sermons warned against modernistic churches and their teachings. At the same time, anyone who reads early CRC magazines, books, sermons, and autobiographies will be struck with the stalwart faith, genuine piety, deep trust, and sacrificial generosity of those generations. Their faith and devotion were at the heart of the CRC community. Flawed and fallible sinners that they were, if the apostle Paul had written letters to them he would, no doubt, have begun with "To the saints in Paterson . . ." or Pella, or Portland, and all the congregations in between.

Volga, South Dakota, CRC

The CRC struggled for many years with "worldly amusements"—especially the trio of movies, dancing, and card playing. The battle was launched in 1928 when synod approved a report that virtually forbade participation in these three amusements. Church councils were mandated to warn unceasingly against these evils and "where repeated admonitions by the consistory are left unheeded, to apply discipline as a last resort."

Although elders were not eager to apply discipline, in some churches young people who refused to renounce dancing and movie attendance were not allowed to make profession of faith. For thirty years the church tried to interpret and enforce the mandate. Eventually the increased popularity of television and films like *The Sound of Music* rendered the 1928 decision unenforceable. In 1966 synod approved a report, "The Film Arts and the Church," spelling an end to the prohibition.

Along with parents, the church also had an educational role. Children were expected to attend worship services as soon as they could sit quietly (and sometimes before that!). Sunday school, at first considered an American novelty, was accepted in most churches by the 1920s. Children's messages and "children's church" did not become commonplace until the 1970s. Young people studied the Heidelberg Catechism, considered the primary tool for educating them in Christian doctrine and living. In their late teens, they were also encouraged to attend a "confession class" with a view to making "profession of faith." Those who were so inclined would meet with the elders and be examined as to their doctrinal knowledge and Christian behavior. If affirmed, they would then make a "public profession" before

observance described below. At the same time, some congregations still use the same order of worship that took shape in the 1930s.

Sunday Observance

One distinguished CRC tradition has been strict observance of the Lord's day, or as it was often called, "Sabbath observance." Basic to "Sabbath observance" was attendance at both Sunday worship services. The rest of the day also was carefully regulated. Members of the CRC were to abstain from working at their regular jobs, except for works of mercy (as in the case of doctors and nurses) or necessity (milking cows), and limit other activities as well. In our family we peeled potatoes and polished shoes on Saturday evening and refrained from bike riding (except to church). Using the car apart from church activities was frowned upon as "joy-riding." Children's activities also were restricted. Playing catch was permitted, but playing a ball game was not. When television came into homes, it remained off on Sunday. A common custom appreciated by parents and children alike was the visit to Grandma's house after one of the services, with treats for all. The children spent time with their cousins, and the women and men (in separate rooms) discussed politics and family and the preacher's sermon— the men often amid clouds of cigar smoke.

Spiritual Nurture of Youth

Parents in CRC homes generally assumed major responsibility for the spiritual training of their children and youth. In nearly all homes Scripture reading and prayer at mealtimes was standard practice. The reading usually followed a Genesis to Revelation pattern, one chapter at a time. In some families evening prayers also were an important source of spiritual formation.

THE TRAINING OF MINISTERS

Ministers who emigrated from the Netherlands were academically well trained. However, in the early years of the CRC, the schooling of ministers was quite minimal. Young men who aspired to the ministry would go to the home of one of the ministers, who would teach them everything they knew about biblical studies and theology, as well as a smattering of Greek and Hebrew—all of this instruction taking place in Dutch. In 1867 this training became more formalized with the establishing of the *Theologische School* in Grand Rapids. Now Calvin Theological Seminary, this school is still the only official CRC institution for training its ministers.

the congregation. In addition to catechism classes, most churches also encouraged young people's societies—devoted at least in part to Bible study.

Christian schools formed the third side of the triangle of the CRC approach to spiritual formation of children and youth. Even though not all CRC communities had such schools, the home-church-school triangle was considered the optimum model.

Calvin Seminary class, 1910

The main change in theological education from the early years is the rigor of the education. Since 1907, seminary students were required to have completed four years of college. Until the 1950s, nearly all seminary students attended Calvin College, where virtually all pre-seminary courses were prescribed, with a heavy concentration in foreign languages, including Latin, Dutch, and Greek. Over time the seminary curriculum came to include a strong emphasis in biblical studies, using Hebrew and Greek, and in theology and church history. This "classical" theological training

The role of the minister is very important to the life of most congregations. Ministry consultants observe that congregational histories often are divided by pastoral chapters. The following excerpt (translated from Dutch) from a brief history of Carnes (Iowa) CRC (1904-1943) illustrates that this also was true in Dutch immigrant congregations: "Rev. William Meyer was chosen and called. He immediately accepted, so our vacancy was short. He came to us in early February 1924. He was also our first minister who preached in the language of the land. He served our congregation for five-and-a-half years. During his tenure here, he suffered the loss of the *Juffrouw* (the minister's wife), and in due time took a brand-new one. Rev. Meyer and family left in July 1929. Then followed a vacancy of nearly fourteen months, during which time six calls were extended without results." The complete history lists the calls and declines for each vacancy, the name of the minister who accepted, the number of years and months he served, and his date of departure.

still is discernable at Calvin Seminary today, although modified by more flexible entrance requirements and a variety of program majors. The most visible change at the seminary is the greater diversity in the student body: now including international students, second career (older) folks, persons of color—and females as well as males.

Today, for those who aspire to the office of minister of the Word, seminary training is followed by six additional steps: endorsement by the seminary board of trustees, declaration of candidacy by the synod, receiving a call from a congregation, accepting a call, examination and approval by a classis, and a service of ordination by the calling congregation.

Worship

The liturgy of the early years was taken over virtually unchanged from the Dutch secessionist churches. (For a "reconstruction" of an early worship service, see Michael De Vries and Harry Boonstra, *Pillar Church in the Van Raalte Era*, Pillar Christian Reformed Church, 2003, chapter 5.) It was a very simple liturgy in which the congregation sang psalms, brought their offerings, and listened to the preacher. The preacher's role included reading the Ten Commandments, the Apostles' Creed, and the Bible passages; leading in prayers; and, of course, preaching the sermon.

Among the first generation, the custom was for women to be seated in the center of the church and the men on the sides. Later the seating became more "American" and families sat together. One important and unfortunate exception was that the young men of the congregation usually sat in the back of the church or the balcony. Their behavior often left much to be desired, sometimes prompting the minister to interrupt his sermon with a stern word to the offenders. In some instances elders and others were stationed strategically to keep order. Another seating practice, now disappeared, was the renting of pews to families, as a

Fulton, Illinois, Ladies' Aid, 1930s

method of collecting funds for the church. Offerings were collected in pouches at the end of long poles, which the deacons lifted over heads and hats with more or less dexterity.

Sermons usually lasted about one hour, and were considered the main element in the worship service. A typical sermon had three points, usually ending with a *toepassing,* the application to people's lives. "Doctrinal" sermons, focusing on Reformed teachings, were more common than they are today, especially since one sermon every Sunday was to be based on a section of the Heidelberg Catechism. The prayers were fewer but longer than today. For example, there was no specific prayer for forgiveness and assurance of pardon, or a prayer of illumination before the sermon. All the petitions and thanksgiving tended to be combined in the "long prayer"—a correct designation. Until the 1930s singing in public worship was limited to the singing of psalms—that is, versifications in Dutch and English based on the biblical book of Psalms. The first *Psalter Hymnal* was published in 1934, to be followed by two later editions—each including an increased number of songs and hymns.

At some undetermined time CRC folks initiated the "peppermint ritual." At the beginning of the sermon the mother would send peppermints down the row, one for each member of the family. Sometimes the courtesy also was extended to nearby guests. Older members took pains to transfer the mint from hand to mouth as surreptitiously as possible. Periodically a child would remove the mint and study how much was left. In some families, mints were distributed to match the points of the sermon— usually three. The custom still is alive and well in some CRC churches, with King and Wilhelmina brands the most popular. Perhaps some observant reader will see fit to enter the peppermint ritual into ecumenical liturgical history.

The Minister Yesterday	The Minister Today
Only formally educated or most highly educated member of the congregation	One of many educated persons, including persons with other advanced degrees
Dressed formally	Dresses casually
Greeted as *Dominee* (a Dutch term of respect) or Rev. [last name]	Greeted as Pastor [last name] or Pastor [first name]
Emphasis on strong doctrinal sermons	Emphasis on call to faith and mission
Solo pastor, no other paid staff	Senior pastor and ministry staff
High value on annual *huizbezoek* (home visiting) of all members	High value on equipping and supporting others for providing pastoral care
Wife was stay-at-home mother and homemaker	Spouse is free to pursue a career outside of home and family responsibilities
Parsonage	Housing allowance

The Lord's Supper was administered four times a year, with the preceding Sunday devoted to a solemn examination and preparation for the sacrament. In the early years, congregants followed the Dutch custom of groups coming forward to sit around a table for receiving the bread and drinking wine from a common cup. As congregations became more Americanized, they discontinued sitting at tables, and elders distributed the elements to the people as they remained in the pews. After the 1918 influenza epidemic the common cup was exchanged for small individual cups. In time, wine has been replaced with grape juice in virtually all congregations.

In the early years the order of worship among the congregations tended to be very similar. In 1916, however, synod was asked to make a thorough appraisal of worship practices, especially since some congregations were adopting American practices too uncritically. Synod appointed a committee to study the matter. Twelve years later Synod 1928 adopted a drastically revised liturgy and declared that it was mandatory for all the churches. The reaction was mostly negative, so at the very next synod—1930—the mandate was reversed. Decades later, in 1968, a CRC liturgical committee presented a long and thorough report to synod, including a recommended (not mandated) order of worship. The report was well received by the congregations but did not bring uniformity. In recent years a host of other worship practices and traditions have been introduced, from weekly communion to praise bands to semicharismatic services.

Growth of the CRC				
	Congregations	Pastors	Families	Members
1857	4	1	130 (est)	600 (est)
1875	26	15	1,500 (est)	7,525
1897	130	85	9,262	49,260
1917	237	169	17,450	89,257
1937	286	260	24,604	117,972
1957	495	392	47,991	211,454
1977	706	661	6,295	288,024
1997	987	Not listed	73,323	285,864
2005	993	Not listed	74,507	273,220

——Based on the annual CRC Yearbook

How Did Isolation Become a Barrier?

The tight social fabric of the Dutch immigrant communities had two consequences: it gave cohesion to the CRC community and simultaneously separated congregations from races and ethnicities different than themselves. (An early exception was the inclusion of some twenty German-speaking congregations in the midwestern United States.)

Obviously, one element of this was the community's continuing "Dutchness." The CRC dropped the *Hollandsche* part of its denominational name fairly early but found it much harder to shake its Dutch identity. The directories of older CRC congregations are loaded with surnames like De Jong and De Vries, and lists of prefixes like Van, Vande, Vanden, and Vander. One method of evangelism was for the "missionary" pastor to go to a town, check the telephone book for Dutch names, and call with this invitation: "We're starting a new CRC church, and we thought you'd like to join." I remember an experience in the 1960s when our Chicago-area congregation had received new members who were Italian and had a Roman Catholic background. When we announced this glad news to the annual "church visitors," the response was, "But do they attend evening services? We're not interested in letting 'once-ers' come into our church."

In this context, whoever came up with the line "If you're not Dutch, you're not much" hadn't considered how insulting this was to persons of other backgrounds and religious traditions. Certainly an "us and them" mentality existed for many generations—so much so that when a Christian Reformed young woman married a Bible-believing man from another denomination, third- and fourth-generation Dutch immigrants would sigh, "She's marrying an outsider."

Midland Park (New Jersey) Christian School

Another dimension of these two consequences, cohesion and exclusion, has been the educational tradition of the CRC. Its strong commitment to Christian education, from kindergarten through college, has been a remarkable achievement and testimony to both educational ideals and sacrificial giving. This tradition also tended to knit the community even closer together. For years the students at Christian day schools were nearly all from Christian Reformed churches. Children from other Christian traditions who attended the schools sometimes felt less than welcome. The more recent broadening of student bodies to include evangelicals and children from unchurched homes has come about largely because of declining enrollments from CRC families. The same is true of Calvin College. In 1936 the Board of Trustees agreed that "the Faculty and the Board are alive to the danger created by the presence of these [non-CRC] students, and are constantly and seriously struggling with this problem." Even as late as 1966 the student body was 93 percent CRC. (This percentage has changed radically in recent years; in 2003 the percentage of CRC students at Calvin fell below 50 percent for the first time.)

The theology and traditions of the CRC, its customs and mores, and no doubt its biases and prejudices, all played a role in its religious and cultural isolation from the American context for generations.

Whether the CRC was more or less isolationist than other immigrant churches I will leave to sociologists to judge. In any case, we must acknowledge that the CRC did not live up to Christ's mandate that there should be no walls, no barriers between those who bear the name Christian. At the same time, I praise God that "by faith I am a member of Christ, and so I share in his anointing" (Heidelberg Catechism, answer 32). I thank God that he brought me to faith through the Christian Reformed Church. And I am thankful that the CRC is becoming more inclusive and diverse in its congregational and denominational life.

DISCUSSION STARTERS

1. How may the Dutch church secession of 1834 have influenced the character of the CRC?

2. Have you experienced or witnessed language controversies in a church? How were they resolved?

3. Are Christian schools a help or a hindrance to reaching out and embracing our neighbors? Explain.

4. How has Sunday observance changed in your family or community in the past fifty years? Evaluate whether this has been a change for better or worse.

5. Do you favor worship that is as uniform as possible in the CRC, or should every congregation determine its own worship style? Why?

6. How has your congregation become more open to diversity in the last twenty years?

CHAPTER THREE

THE CRC OF CANADA AND ITS RELATIONSHIPS

Louis M. Tamminga

"Accept one another, then, just as Christ accepted you, in order to bring praise to God."
—Romans 15:7

The CRC denominational office building in Grand Rapids, Michigan, proudly flies three flags on its modest campus. The middle one is the flag of the church: the triangle representing the triune God and the cross of salvation. This flag is flanked by two national flags: one for the United States, the other for Canada.

The CRC is a binational church. About three-fourths of its membership resides south of the 3,987 mile (6,479 km) border, which mostly follows the 49th parallel; the other one-fourth of its membership lives north of this border. The two nations that host this one denomination have been at peace since the War of 1812. The two segments of the CRC have been mostly at peace too. Their union dates back to a century ago when Alberta settlers were organized into some small CRC congregations. The vast majority of the Canadian Dutch immigrant churches were established in the 1940s and 1950s on the heels of World War II.

HOW DUTCH AND "REFORMED" WERE THEY?

Most of the settlers who joined the CRC in Canada had been members of the *Gereformeerde Kerken in Nederland* (GKN), though several came from other Reformed denominations. The GKN was formed in 1892 from a merger of two

A traditional country church in the Netherlands

small denominations that had separated from the historical church of the sixteenth century Reformation, the *Nederlands Hervormde Kerk* (NHK). The NHK had gradually become theologically liberal, motivating these two smaller groups of congregations to leave its fellowship.

From its inception, the new GKN denomination did well. Whereas earlier generations had been mostly simple folk, their children enjoyed more educational privileges and economic opportunities. By the beginning of the twentieth century the denomination had become an important player on the national scene. GKN leaders in church and society had a keen cultural understanding, and were among the Netherlands' contributing citizens.

However, as the people of the GKN increased in prosperity—though modest by today's standards—they also increased in their materialism. Conflict and infighting among the denominational leaders became a sad reality. Increased pursuit of doctrine was not matched by increased delight in godliness. Moralism and legalism crept into the church. Theological interest remained enviably high, but it was channeled more into rational discussion than mutual edification in the Lord. Theologians argued, and theological camps were formed.

An important fact that is sometimes overlooked in understanding Dutch attitudes is that for centuries the Netherlands was one of the larger colonial powers in the world. For over three hundred years it administrated the sprawling three-hundred-island archipelago of Indonesia, stretching 3,500 miles from east to west with some 100 million inhabitants. Deep in the Dutch consciousness there was a quiet pride of belonging to a nation that was regarded by other nations as a world power. I am convinced that this reality instilled in the Dutch an undeniable self-perception of national and racial superiority.

Other realities in Dutch national life also played a role. The Great Depression of the 1930s brought unemployment into many homes. As a result, class distinctions—never totally absent from Dutch society—became even more pronounced.

The Depression was followed closely by World War II (1939-1945). From 1940 to the end of the war, the Netherlands was occupied by the Nazi German military. By the grace of God, many GKN communities embodied the spiritual strength

Following the 1960s, some 2 ½ million immigrants settled in the Netherlands. They came mostly from Indonesia, The Dutch Antilles, Surinam, and the Muslim world of the Near East. The "Samen op Weg Kerken" (GKN, HKN, and Lutheran Church; they have since merged into the Protestantse Kerken van Nederland) published a statement on the state of race relations within their ranks. The report, *Born in Zion*, states that racism is manifested in feelings of superiority and in "cramped" attitudes toward non-Western people. It notes that many immigrants from Indonesia initially joined the various Reformed denominations, but that most of them have left. Subdued racism is one reason, says the report. But another reason is that non-Western members experience the transcendental in the Christian faith, whereas for the white Dutch, faith is mostly a matter of agreement to reasoning. "White churches," says the report, "have become closed communities. What applies to immigrants applies to newcomers in general."

Dutch harbor scene

required to serve in the forefront of opposing Nazism. During those anxious years, their worship services reached new depths of communing with God and with each other. But the GKN also faced problems. On the national scene, public morality suffered during the chaotic war years, and members of the GKN were not immune. Also, doctrinal disputes racked the organizational life of the GKN. In 1944, the darkest year of the war, yet another church split took place, piercing straight through families and resulting in pain and alienation still felt today.

"My grandparents came to Alberta before the war. . . . Many communities were then ethnically defined: British, German, Polish, Scandinavian, Dutch. . . . Such communities are now more broadly integrated in the general population. . . . Most denominations, and local congregations for that matter, have an ethnic flavor."

All of these historical factors had an effect on the new immigrants who came to Canada in the late 1940s and 1950s. They felt a deep sense of freedom in their new country. They had high hopes for economic improvement. Even in their new environment they remained assertive people and held to their strong convictions. They were a quietly proud people, dependable and frugal. They faced hardships with endurance, as the generations before them had done in their former homeland. There was a stubborn streak in them. Sometimes personal relationships were strained, but they still remained faithful to their new congregations.

Race and racial reconciliation was a topic seldom discussed by these immigrants, but in later generations their children and grandchildren would observe that at a visceral level their parents held views that would be considered race prejudice or even racist today.

WHAT DIFFERENCE DOES AN OCEAN MAKE?

Already during the late 1950s Canadian immigrants began to notice changes in the outlook of their relatives across the Atlantic Ocean. The upheaval of World War II left in its wake a questioning of traditional biblical certainties, a weakening of Christian discipleship, and a yearning for pleasure and material goods. Church attendance declined sharply; many young people deserted completely. The Heidelberg Catechism, the Church Order, and even the Ten Commandments were seen as antiquated documents. Dutch hosts found their visiting relatives from Canada narrow-minded and "behind the times." The longtime rich relationship between the theological faculty of the Free University of Amsterdam and the faculty of Calvin Theological Seminary lost its luster.

All of this is, admittedly, a generalization. There were (and still are) many local churches in the Netherlands where devout ministers preached the Word of God faithfully and where people walked humbly with their God. And GKN people have been and continue to be very generous toward those in need at home and abroad. Nevertheless, the changes in the Netherlands had an impact on the CRC in Canada.

In some Canadian CRC circles there was a retrenching toward conservatism, perhaps in an effort to avoid the erosion that had paralyzed so many Dutch churches. Most churches soon learned, however, that their efforts did not and could not turn back the clock. They discovered that the Word of God is not static but dynamic, always affording new insights and fresh applications in changing situations. At the annual synodical meetings, Canadian delegates often pleaded for a mildly progressive direction. For example, women have been elected to church office in most Canadian congregations—certainly at a higher percentage than in their U.S. counterparts.

The Canadian churches also grew in another way. They became more intentional in their faithfulness to God's Word and the confessions; they stressed that the fundamentals of faith and godly practice were not negotiable.

How Did They Affirm the Kingdom in a New Land?

People often wonder what caused these Dutch folks to pull up stakes and move to a new land.

Without doubt, economic factors were a prominent consideration. But parents who had emigrated also would often refer to their children: "We did it for the future of our children." As the years went by, they began to see the vertical element more clearly: in God's providence they and their children were called to serve God in this great land. Their churches meant a lot to them. So when the early immigrants became grandparents, they could be found at Christian school society meetings, and they remained regular contributors.

Post-war Canada faced many challenges and offered many possibilities. Following the peace of 1945, large numbers of demobilized soldiers from the agrarian sector enrolled at Canadian colleges with government support. This resulted in a shortage of farm labor, which led to recruiting farm laborers from Western Europe to fill the void. In 1952, the Canadian government opened the door for people with other skills and professions as well.

Immigrants peering through the windows of a train

One reality the immigrant churches had to face was that the Canadian society took little note of them. In their initial years, therefore, the churches became social rallying places for the immigrant communities. Amid the harsh realities of society's indifference, the churches were islands of security and predictability. Absorbed as church members were in building an economic base, there was a mild sense of competition among the churches. But once the misfortunes in their circles had been identified, congregations readily came to each other's rescue, sometimes at considerable cost.

As helpful as this sense of belonging was, it had its negative face as well. Church leaders often defended their congregational goals and practices based on personal comfort rather than godly vision. They were easily threatened by unfamiliar changes. The style of discussion in church circles was not inquiring and exploratory so much as declaratory and quickly contentious. Disputes and conflicts erupted with some regularity, and personal slights were not always readily forgiven or forgotten.

It's true that these immigrants were busy people with much on their minds. Economic safety nets were by and large unknown in Canadian society. No wonder they didn't read much or keep especially current with Canadian affairs! Their established Canadian neighbors who belonged to mainline denominations expressed their religious convictions cautiously, and scarcely applied them to life in society. On the other hand, neighbors who belonged to evangelical denominations expressed their convictions more eloquently, which these newer immigrants found a bit daunting. The early immigrant churches did not radiate welcoming hospitality. The few "Canadians" who did join them, mostly by reason of marrying a member from these arcane communities, soon realized that becoming fully accepted would take a while— a long while.

The early immigrants had not come from a church culture where evangelism was a priority. So it is no surprise that evangelism was not a high value in the new congregations in Canada either. Nor were they much inclined to participate in ministering to Canada's social problems. Given this overall climate, it is really quite remarkable that

Immigrant congregations included many children

concerted efforts in the areas of politics and labor go as far back as the early 1950s. Even more remarkable, the credit needs to go primarily to a handful of visionaries whose trailblazing ministry found backing from only a limited number of CRC folks.

Still, these early immigrant settlers were people of the Word. They were Calvinists. They knew that the gospel had to be shared and that the Christian faith required expression in broader life. And even though meaningful contacts with the Canadian scene remained limited during their lifetime, they planted the seeds of a more fully-orbed Christian lifestyle.

ARE WE OUR PARENTS' CHILDREN?

"My husband and I were young children when we came to Canada. . . . We all worked hard on the family farm. . . . My parents were never effuse in expressing their faith but we knew that their decisions were guided by faith. . . . Our parents loved us kids a lot. . . . Our own children like the traditional worship style but they are more open about their faith."

Many of the immigrants who came to Canada were young families. Single people, however, also were numerous. In short order, many of these immigrants bought farms and worked eagerly to pay them off. Teenage sons and daughters joined the family work force or found jobs to augment family income. Some of them who spent their teenage years in the field felt robbed of an education. Few remember vacations with their parents. Family life under these circumstances was not always conducive to establishing friendships with "Canadian" young people.

But as the new generations assumed their adult place among the settlers, church communities became more balanced. Church life matured; changes for the better were accepted, though hesitantly. Congregations found their own identity, and members took more pride in congregational life.

Those of the second or third generations sometimes mention that their parents were sparse in expressing love. Yet deep down they know that their immigrant grandparents and parents loved them and wanted "the best" for them.

The generations born in Canada were inevitably different from the early settlers. Their knowledge of the "old country" mostly was secondhand. There was no Great Divide between the settlers and their children, but there was a disconnect that often left the settlers lonely and sad—although they expressed it rarely.

In some ways it is a marvel—and a joy—that the kingdom idea gradually gained some prominence among the children of immigrants. The notion that, among other reasons, Reformed believers of Dutch origin had come to Canada for the sake of the kingdom gained new emphasis.

CANADIAN, EH?

The last three decades have brought many changes to CRC communities in Canada. Congregations have matured further. The Dutch accent is not heard as much in council meetings. And council meetings have become more outward directed. Musically talented members are leading in worship services. Many children and grandchildren of immigrants are college and university graduates who have excelled in business and professions. They are no longer aliens in the land. Evangelism is more readily accepted as an earnest challenge. "Canadians" who have been grafted into Dutch

"When I was in college, I stopped going to church. . . . Spiritually I was in a dry place. . . . For a time I attended the United Church; nice people, flaky preaching . . . then the Baptist Church; good people, sweet preaching. . . . I have now been back several years in the CRC . . . . I have come to appreciate the depth of the Reformed faith; it has the mettle to address the cultural issues in Canadian society."

Generation to generation

"My wife and I have been members of this church for seven years. We are sixth generation Scottish. . . . We feel at home in our congregation. . . . The preaching is biblical, confessional, and practical. Many members here are Dutch, but for us that means no more than that their names are Dutch."

immigrant family trees are feeling reasonably at home.

Many new church buildings have been erected in recent years, some with architectural beauty. Imaginative initiatives have brightened the sense of mission in the churches. Here are a few examples:

- "Sea to Sea with the CRC" bike tour of 2005

- Small group ministry rallies for women

- "Service Link" facilitating volunteer labor

- Generous giving worldwide to those in need, including tsunami victims in Indonesia and hurricane relief in the United States

- Participation of young people in work teams has strengthened CRC mission efforts abroad

Today, the windows on communities surrounding the churches in Canada are being opened a little further every year. Deacons have taken the lead in ministering to their neighborhoods. These significant developments deserve separate mention:

- The Christian day school movement in Canada made a strong contribution to Christian life and aided Christian social awareness and action across the land. Christian curriculum studies even benefited the national educational systems. The Institute for Christian Studies in Toronto, which traces its beginnings back to 1956—became widely recognized as a first-rate institution of higher education. Two regional Christian colleges, King's University College in Edmonton, Alberta (1979), and Redeemer College in Ancaster, Ontario (1982), enjoy fine reputations far beyond the boundaries of the CRC.

  Perhaps it is no surprise that CRC campus ministers are located strategically on many of Canada's college and university campuses. These ministries to CRC youth and others are supported eagerly by the area classis and neighboring churches.

- *Christian Courier* (formerly *Calvinist Contact*)—a fine periodical—has consistently brought the Christian vision into many homes. In addition, *The Banner,* the synodically sponsored denominational magazine of the CRC, has also been sensitive to Canadian aspirations, thanks in no small part to effective editors who were themselves Canadian. All these institutions and efforts have contributed significantly toward the articulation of a Calvinistic world-and-life view.

- The Christian Labor Association of Canada (CLAC) organized its first local labor union in the early 1950s. CLAC engaged in a large amount of research to come to a clearer understanding of a Christian approach

- "The CRC must not lose its Canadian identity, but I also feel that there is much strength in being part of a binational denomination."

- "CRC members in Canada are proud of what they accomplished through their Christian institutions . . . they feel that the CRC churches are less equipped to engage Canada as a nation, since the U.S. segment has little appreciation for it."

- "Canadian culture is like a quilt, less a melting pot."

- "The CRC of Canada must continue to find its own style and identity but remain with the CRC of the U.S."

toward economic enterprise and labor relations. Its courageous efforts, often in the face of daunting opposition, were rewarded with legal certification in l961. CLAC is still going strong today with offices located across Canada.

- Parallel concerns in the political arena led to the formation of the Committee for Public Justice (CPJ). CPJ has spoken with impact into the political arena, serving the nation with distinction. At the same time, implementing the vision for an authentic Christian political party has proved to be very complex. Although some attempts have been made, a full-fledged Christian political party has not become a reality.

- CRC leaders in Canada contributed significantly toward the chaplaincy ministry practice and its philosophical underpinnings—both academically and institutionally—across Canada.

- Christian care facilities for elderly members have sprung up in many places.

- Christian farmers and business people have added their efforts to come to Christian understanding and practice in their areas of agriculture and other forms of enterprise.

WHAT'S UNIQUE ABOUT THE CRC IN CANADA?

In the late 1940s and 1950s, when the CRC sent "home missionaries" to Canada to enfold the new settlers, it was simply assumed that the new congregations would be part of one denomination—the CRC of North America. After all, the small tribe of CRC congregations that emerged in Canada in earlier generations were organizationally

one with those in the U.S. Today some 27 percent of all CRC members reside in Canada, the other 73 percent in the U.S. The CRC is organized into 47 classes (plural of *classis,* the Reformed term for a regional cluster of congregations), of which twelve are located in Canada and thirty-five in the U.S.

As Canadian leaders began to focus more on the binational reality of the one denomination, the issue of national imbalance became more problematic. At the same time, there was a growing understanding of differences between the CRC in the U.S. and the CRC in Canada. Some compared it to an elephant sharing a room with a mouse: the elephant pays little attention to the mouse, while the mouse watches every move of the elephant. Some people began to question whether the denominational governance that appears mostly aligned with one country can do full justice to the membership in another country.

A number of developments kept this question on the front burner. The Kuyperian kingdom vision brought by the earlier generation of immigrants to Canada began to be embraced by a new generation. In large part this was the result of vigorous research conducted in the Christian educational

Who is my neighbor?

systems, the organizations for Christian social action, and in the regional diaconal bodies in Canada. The denominational Christian Reformed World Relief Committee (CRWRC), founded in 1962, met an enthusiastic response in Canada. Soon its Canadian chapters generated their own plethora of activities on a national and international scale. Today 40 percent of the overall CRWRC budget is funded from Canadian sources.

The conviction that CRC Canada needed some form of leadership structures of its own led to the formation of the Council of Christian Reformed Churches in Canada (CCRCC) in 1968. Composed of delegates from the twelve Canadian classes, the council served the Canadian churches with admirable effectiveness for some three decades. In the late 1970s an administrative facility was erected in Burlington, Ontario, to better support CRC Canada ministry. A more suitable building was erected in 1986 that still serves CRC Canada efficiently today. Huge quantities of CRC publications and communications are mailed from the Burlington office to every part of Canada.

The CCRCC soon became a deliberative body, addressing numerous issues on the Canadian scene. Its many committees and task forces produced position papers that are still being consulted. Its Committee for Contact with the Government sent numerous testimonies to the national and provincial governments of Canada. CCRCC also initiated ministries to native Canadian communities in Winnipeg, Manitoba; and Regina, Saskatchewan.

But the CCRCC had one drawback. It had no recognized ecclesiastical standing. The regular flow of church concerns from local consistories to the annual synods mostly bypassed CCRCC. And the council's many ministries had to be financed from a "ministry share" over and above the congregations' per family "ministry shares" to the denomination.

In order to obviate these problems, Synod 1997 replaced CCRCC with the Canadian Ministries

Board. Its mandate was to supervise denominational ministries in Canada and international ministries on behalf of CRC Canada. The new board was to function under the larger umbrella of the denominational Board of Trustees (BOT). That arrangement also proved unsatisfactory, particularly because of ongoing confusion about the relationship between the two boards.

After many back-and-forth deliberations, Synod 2000 implemented yet another plan. It reconstituted the CRC Board of Trustees as a smaller but truly binational board with fifteen members from Canada and fifteen from the U.S. On behalf of synod this board was mandated to guide and supervise all denominational ministries and whatever matters might properly be on its agenda. Each segment was duly incorporated under Canadian and American law. The Canadian part of the BOT was given the freedom to meet separately and to deliberate on ministry challenges and responsibilities peculiarly Canadian.

This restructured Board of Trustees is generally thought to go a long way toward meeting the needs and challenges of CRC Canada. In 2002, for example, it organized a Canada-wide conference in Edmonton, Alberta, which generated a great deal of enthusiasm and ministry initiatives.

Some Canadian leaders remain convinced, however, that a binational church arrangement will always detract from the CRC Canada's national identity. The (now defunct) Canada Council's meetings had a Canadian feel to them. The council was a decision-making body, but it was also a platform to reflect on Canadian issues that, they say, the present BOT lacks.

Others are quick to point out, however, that denominational unity has been a blessing to both Canada and the U.S.: it has deepened insight, multiplied initiatives, and added to ministry strength. Canadian delegates were at times able to bridge the divide between progressives and conservatives by articulating a neo-Kuyperian vision. U.S. delegates impressed Canadian delegates with their

"Our ministries must stem from our common citizenship in the kingdom of heaven. . . . Only from that source can both segments of the CRC become more humane and caring both at home and on the world stage. . . . Only then can they fight the spirits of secularism and consumerism among them. . . ."

"In the Canadian context, the CRC needs to address and/or be involved in social justice issues, ministry with the poor and aboriginal peoples, interchurch relations, and interaction with governments. Further, Canadian law requires that Canadian government bodies maintain 'direction, supervision, and control' over receipted tax deductible funds gathered in Canada. Because of the binational character of the CRC, Canadians must have significant ownership and authority for planning and managing ministry in Canada."
—From a report of the CRC Board of Trustees to Synod 2000

"I have always felt that the Canadian CRC should have grown into an independent Canadian denomination. . . . Our ministries would have reflected more fully the realities of Canadian history, outlook, identity, and government. . . . With a national ministry center we would have attracted more well-educated young members to remain closely involved in various types of ministry truly in touch with national needs."

organizational savvy and godly devotion to the church's callings. At the same time, Canadians sometimes wonder why Americans don't seem to know much about Canada. (Quick, what's the name of the Prime Minister of Canada?)

Patterns in church life, of course, never separate as neatly as one might surmise. Both the U.S. and Canada have been influenced by evangelicalism, subjectivism, and the charismatic movement. Both also have been affected by secularism, materialism, and consumerism. The entire denomination has witnessed profound changes in worship styles. Canadian churches have had their own problems in dealing with doctrinal controversies. In fact, proportionately, recent congregational splits hit the CRC in Canada harder than in the U.S.: twenty-five congregations in Canada compared to fifty in the U.S.

Maranatha CRC, Lethbridge, Alberta

WHAT'S HAPPENING NOW?

On both sides of the border, CRC members are focusing more on the ministries of their local churches than on the overall ministry of the denomination. At the same time local churches are finding it harder to maintain the loyalty of individual members. Members seem to transfer easily to other denominations without much soul-searching. Congregations have to "earn" the loyalty of younger members. Neither segment of the denomination is witnessing vigorous membership growth. Though the CRC in Canada and in the U.S. tend to assess international developments differently, they agree that widespread evil and violence are indicators that the end times are approaching, and that ecclesiastical unity and close cooperation add strength to a common witness. Existing CRC governance provisions hold promise for effective cooperation between the church in Canada and the U.S.

Many of the issues confronting the churches on both sides of the border are similar. The information age opened the doors of our homes and hearts to a mishmash of sensate ideologies and hedonistic enticement. Materialism and permissiveness will remain formidable enemies of the CRC generations to come. Only a combination of godliness and earnest biblical teaching will keep the new generations in Canada and the U.S. on the path of life.

Evangelicalism will probably be a major influence in our churches on both sides of the border, though perhaps somewhat more in the U.S. than in Canada. Whatever the reality, pietistic and spiritualistic leanings everywhere must be counterbalanced by a sustained effort to adorn all human activities with kingdom loyalty. This does not mean that piety and spirituality are not to be prized in themselves. It does mean that we are called to be the Lord's good stewards across the entire spectrum of human activities. It is not enough to decry the loss of "Reformed" understanding and commitment. This generation must demonstrate to the next what "Reformed" really means and why it is important for us in personal and family life and in the public arena.

Finally, let's agree that the CRC in Canada and in the U.S. need each other. Let's give each other space and neither underestimate nor overestimate the differences. A functional unity results as much from one common Source as from one common task. Let us live and share the good news of the Master, and let us be godly earth-keepers and caretakers for the Master in all life's compartments. Those who are involved in the Master's service have more reason for optimism regarding the future than those who are not. All of this is expressed eloquently by the mission statement of the CRC:

> As people called by God we gather to praise God, listen to him, and respond. We love and care for one another as God's people. We commit ourselves to serve and to tell others about Jesus. We pursue God's justice and peace in every area of life.

DISCUSSION STARTERS

1. The Dutch settlers to the U.S. in the 1800s preserved the use of the Dutch language for several generations. The Dutch settlers to Canada, a century later, switched over to English within a few years. What do you think accounts for the difference?

2. During its first fifty years the CRC in the U.S. remained fairly isolated from the national scene. In what ways was this different for CRC Canada?

3. Reflect on your personal social circle: to what extent is it limited to CRC people? How do you and your congregation influence the wider community?

4. What are some of the main things you received from the moral arsenal of your parents? Did that arsenal include any forms of race prejudice? How has your impact on your children differed from your parents' impact on you?

5. Is the membership of your church multiethnic or multiracial? What can persons from your tradition or culture do to help persons from another tradition or culture be more "at home"?

6. It is generally thought that Canadian news outlets cover a lot more news about the U.S. than U.S. news outlets report about Canada. Why might this be?

CHAPTER FOUR

FIRST AMERICANS IN THE CRC: THE LAST FIFTY YEARS

Alfred E. Mulder

" . . . one God and Father of all, who is over all and through all and in all." —Ephesians 4:6

Thirty-five miles north of the Zuni pueblo and bordering the Navajo nation in every direction, Gallup, New Mexico, is the self-proclaimed Indian Capital of the World. With Rehoboth Christian School nestled nearby, Gallup is also the geographic hub for a dozen and a half Christian Reformed congregations. The majority of the congregations are Navajo, a few are mostly white, and one is predominantly Zuni.

My young family and I moved to Gallup in February 1968. In May I attended my first "Indian General Conference" meeting in the basement of the old Rehoboth church building. One circle of chairs was gathered around tables in the center of the room; a second circle of chairs was arranged along the wall. Imagine my surprise to see the inner circle—with one or two exceptions—occupied by white missionaries, and the outer circle—without exception—occupied by Native American workers. The dialogue for the day was equally dominated by white missionaries.

In the late 1800s, simultaneous with waning military resistance by American Indians, the U.S. government decided to "civilize the savage." The weapon of choice was the boarding school, by which children were isolated from their families and immersed in white culture. Early in this effort the government appealed to churches to assist in this cultural assault.

It was in this climate that the Christian Reformed Church debated doing mission work among Indians in the southwest. Initial efforts among the Sioux in South Dakota had gone poorly, adding weight to the general fear that work among Native Americans would be fruitless. Would Native Americans ever accept a white man's religion? Weren't Indians a dying breed? If not, did they have the capacity to become mature Christians and develop "real" Christian Reformed congregations?

In 1896 a "mission-minded" Rev. Johannes Groen visited reservations in the southwestern United States and then convinced synod to send missionaries to the U.S. territories of Arizona and New Mexico (these territories became the 48th and 49th states of the United States in 1912). By October 1896, Herman and Katie Fryling and Andrew and Effa Vander Wagen had begun work

Early missionary assistant Jacob C. Morgan and missionary Leonard P. Brink

in Fort Defiance, Arizona, among the Navajo. One year later the Vander Wagens moved on to the Zuni pueblo.

So began a great missionary cloud of Christian Reformed witnesses—heroes of faith among them. They taught young and old about Jesus—in schools, in Navajo homes and camps, in Zuni pueblos. They established schools in Rehoboth and Zuni to teach life skills along with Christian faith and a hospital for medical care. They trained "Native workers" who helped translate hymns and Scriptures into the language of the people. For generations, by all the means within their grasp, they helped native children and adults come to faith in Jesus. Admittedly they also conveyed a CRC version of white American culture. Yet over the next fifty-plus years a fledgling church began to emerge.

WHAT WOULD AN INDIGENOUS CHURCH LOOK LIKE?

Let's fast-forward to the mid-1950s.

Indian Missions was supervised by the CRC Board of Foreign and Indian Missions, although administered largely by the Indian General Conference (IGC) led by white missionaries. In foreign missions style, the IGC was cut from the same cloth as the Japan General Conference and the Nigeria General Conference. Harry Boer, a CRC missionary in Nigeria, wrote a stinging critique of the work among the Navajo and Zuni—pointing out the failure to raise up more indigenous leaders and the meager fruit in terms of conversion. The dialogue that followed prompted the Board of Foreign and Indian Missions and synod to evaluate their mission principles and practice.

Indigenous Congregations

Synod 1954 affirmed the *ultimate goal* of establishing native churches *"which should be of their own free choice thoroughly Reformed and in full and organic union with the Christian Reformed Church."* The grounds, however, revealed the presumption of white cultural norms: "It is but natural that . . . a church shall seek to establish on the mission field a native church that shall resemble

For a crisp and candid report of these frontier beginnings, see *Flourishing in the Land* by Scott Hoezee and Christopher H. Meehan, pages 1-46. Also see *Navaho and Zuni for Christ*, edited by J.C. De Korne and *Zuni Also Prays* by Cornelius Kuipers.

Synod 1953 adopted a series of statements including these two mission principles:

The missionary is not called to transmit his own culture to the mission field, but to proclaim the Gospel which itself has the power to vitalize all that is good and to exscind all that is evil in the cultural life of the people he serves.

The training of natives for evangelistic work and the development of a native ministry is essential for the building up of an indigenous church.

—*Acts of Synod* 1953, page 85

as closely as possible the sending church." Again, "The Indian people are gradually taking over our own white culture which will eventually replace the Indian cultures. . . ." Consistent with this assimilation intent, synod recommended that Native churches first be granted "an associate relationship" because this would "allow the native church time to develop sufficiently to meet the standards of the Christian Reformed Church Order"(*Acts of Synod* 1942, pp. 82-92).

This ultimate goal was soon put to the test. In 1956 the all-Navajo believers group in Gallup—albeit with a white missionary—became an *associate* CRC congregation. The 1957 Acts of

The first consistory of Bethany Church

Left to right: elder Wilson Barber Sr., deacon Tom Atkinson, pastor Donald E. Houseman, deacon Amos Patrick, elder Steward Barton Sr. Bethany Church in Gallup was the first all-Navajo congregation and the first all non-white congregation to be in "full and organic union" with the CRC. One small step for the Gallup congregation, one giant leap for the CRC!

Synod reports, "December 27, 1956, was a very important day in the annals of our Indian missions. On that day the Gallup Church was formally organized as a congregation and a consistory was elected to take over the responsibility and direction of the church. This church is *associated* (italics added) with Classis Rocky Mountain and after a period of orientation will be received, we trust, into full and regular status as a congregation within our denomination." That trust was soon rewarded. The very next year synod repented of the associate category and encouraged the Gallup church to request classis Rocky Mountain to grant "full status in the Christian Reformed Church" (*Acts of Synod* 1958, pp. 214-215). The congregation and classis happily complied.

Indigenous Leaders

From the earliest days, the white missionaries recruited and trained Navajo and Zuni people to assist in the work—especially with language interpretation and translation. Nevertheless, the transition to Native leaders has been painfully slow. One story that illustrates this painful transition comes from the early 1960s: a Navajo young man studied for a few years at CRC colleges and became an assistant to a highly esteemed white missionary. The young leader was surprised by the missionary's critical spirit toward the people ("You tell them to dig a hole, and if you don't tell them to stop they'll dig all the way to China"). Yet when this young worker authorized a women's Bible study group to invite others, he was reprimanded for acting without permission. Eventually he left the work in frustration, obtained educational degrees, and distinguished himself in another profession. He still is a loyal lay leader in the CRC, but was lost to the profession of his first love.

Periodically synod wrestled with the need for ordained Native leaders. Having decided previously not to recognize the office of evangelist and not to approve ordination limited to the native setting, Synod 1958 saw only two options. One, Native workers could pursue "the regular course of ordination" involving college and seminary. Two, they could hope to qualify by way of an exceptional Church Order provision, that of "possessing exceptional gifts."

The logjam was finally broken in October 1962 when Scott K. Redhouse, a graduate of Cook Christian Training School in Phoenix, was ordained on the basis of "possessing exceptional gifts." This was followed in comparatively rapid succession by the ordination of three Reformed Bible Institute graduates: Scott's older brother Paul, Sampson Yazzie, and Edward Henry. This initial cluster was followed by four more Navajo ministers over the next thirty-plus years, three of them Calvin Seminary graduates (see sidebar). In recent decades additional workers also were ordained as evangelists; yet the need for indigenous leaders remains acute.

Revs. Scott and Paul Redhouse; younger brother Scott left the CRC in 1975 and ministered independently until his death in 1998. Elder brother Paul, who retired in 1990, has continued to provide leadership to the Four Corners CRC in Teec Nos Pos, Arizona.

Navajo Ministers

Scott K. Redhouse
October 1962

Paul H. Redhouse
September 1963

Sampson T. Yazzie
September 1965

Edward Henry
March 1968

Anthony Begay
September 1974

Raymond Slim
October 1994

Stanley Jim
March 1996

Bobby Boyd
November 2004

"Indigenized" Structures

For sixty-seven years mission work among the Navajo and Zuni was administered as a foreign field. Known variously as the Board of Heathen Missions, the Board of Missions, and the Board of Indian and Foreign Missions, curiously in 1958 it was renamed the Board of Foreign Missions. Denominational leaders also began to talk seriously about transferring the "Indian field" from Foreign Missions to Home Missions.

The time was ripe. All "off-reservation" work transferred to Home Missions in 1960. By 1963 synod decided that the historic "reservation" work should also transfer to Home Missions. The report included comments about "the Americanization of the Indian during the last twenty years" and stated that "the Indian has been gradually making a transition from one culture to another." However, the official grounds were mercifully practical: it was consistent with the commitment to establish congregations "in organic union" with the CRC and would unify the administration of all work done both on and off the reservation. The transfer date was January 1, 1964. This change in administration was accompanied by change on the "field" as well. The Rehoboth and Zuni mission schools were included in the transfer, but the Rehoboth hospital was "hived off" to the Luke Society, which was conceived by the Rev. Marvin P. Vander Bosch of Denver for the purpose of extending the ministry of the Rehoboth hospital.

The ordination of the four Navajo pastors emboldened Native leaders as a whole to be more assertive in their voice and role. By 1971 the Indian General Conference had become a coalition of Native and white missionaries. When Home Missions asked them to plan a celebration of the seventy-fifth anniversary of Indian missions, their initial response was, "It's your anniversary; you celebrate it." Eventually, however, local leaders agreed to host a field-wide celebration, including somewhat muted denominational pomp and circumstance.

More change would follow. Gallup elder and Navajo council member Edward T. Begay (see photo p. 84) was elected to the Board of Home Missions and helped expose differing salary scales for white and Native missionaries. By 1975 the Indian General Conference had morphed into a "Council of Indian Churches" with both missionary and lay representatives. In 1981, having approved *the concept* of a "classis of Indian churches" at its previous session, synod—amazingly—also approved a substantial list of requested modifications to the Church Order, including a simplification of the Form of Subscription and the election of elders and deacons (*Acts of Synod* 1981, pp. 14-17).

Students from Rehoboth Christian School, Rebecca Celestine and Janelle Cronin, proudly display the school banner.

Rehoboth includes students from kindergarten through grade 12.

For many CRC mission supporters, the name *Rehoboth* is synonymous with "Indian Missions." Located along Interstate 40 just east of Gallup, Rehoboth Christian School was founded in 1903 by the Christian Reformed Church as a boarding school for Native American students and a ministry to the Native American peoples of the Four Corners region. A day school now, Rehoboth continues its multicultural ministry, serving approximately 60 percent Native American students, 30 percent Anglo students, and 10 percent students of Hispanic origin and other races and ethnicities. Rehoboth's student body also is economically diverse, with 30 percent of the students coming from very low income families.

With these cultural accommodations in hand, Classis Red Mesa was constituted in the fall of 1982 with eleven member congregations. Five of the eleven congregations had organized earlier in the year, and four more were pending. Native Christian leaders were now assured a seat at the inner circle—the table of synod.

The synod of 1980 gave three grounds for approving *in concept* the council's request to organize as a Classis of Indian Churches within the Christian Reformed Church:

a. "[It is] judged that the identity of the Indian churches and their unity with the Christian Reformed Church are both served by the formation of a Classis of Indian Churches.

b. The formation of a Classis of Indian Churches will promote the interdependence of cultures within the Christian Reformed Church.

c. The formation of a Classis of Indian Churches will promote the growth, maturity, and responsibility of the Indian churches."

---Acts of Synod 1980, pages 35-36

CAN I BE NATIVE AMERICAN AND CHRISTIAN?

For Christians who grew up in traditional Navajo settings, becoming a Christian often involved conflict. When Ernest Benally of Farmington, New Mexico, became a Christian, his father rejected him: "Navajo religion is difficult to separate from Navajo culture. In my father's eyes, when I left our religion, I left our culture, identity, and him personally." Rev. Stanley Jim, Home Missions regional leader, also grew up under both traditional Navajo teachings at home and Christian teaching at a boarding school. In his late teens, at a point of deep despair and considering suicide, he remembered words from his Bible teacher: "When you come to the end of your rope, call on God." He was, and he did. Soon after that he came forward at a camp meeting led by his uncle, Rev. Paul Redhouse. "Yet later when I went home," Stanley recalls, "I told my mom and dad that I did something I was happy about: I made a commitment to Christ. My mom said nothing and walked out of the room. My father stayed there and then told me that I had betrayed his teaching."

Other new believers met a mixture of responses:
- James Litson of Teec Nos Pos, Arizona, grew up under "the blessing way" and received Christian instruction at a Presbyterian mission school; he also married a Christian woman. Later when James was struggling with alcoholism, his father encouraged him "to try his wife's faith."
- Marla Jasperse of Fort Wingate, unlike

her mother, was raised as a Christian. Marla said, "People seem to respect my stand for Jesus." In fact, a traditional Navajo woman told her, "You have a God who can make you strong, and you don't have to worry."

- Paul Phillips, now from Albuquerque, said he "was taught from my mom not to practice anything from our Navajo tradition or culture. So in large part we were distanced from our family and sheltered from traditional religious culture."

Zuni experiences varied as well:

- Nina Chimoni was taught to follow Jesus by her mother Olive and her older brother Rex, who also was the mission leader at one point. Nina believes it is important to appreciate your culture and language and traditional values, but "you choose one way, and you stick to it, and do not go back and forth."

- Others, however, reflected on how complex these choices often were in a traditionally religious village. Virginia Chavez sees it this way: "It is common

Virginia Chavez of the Zuni pueblo

knowledge (in the village) that I have taken a stand as a Christian. All new Christians have to go through that. When people know, sometimes they even come and ask me to pray for them."

- Levias Natawa also attended the Zuni mission school and did not participate in the Zuni way. His grandfather Rex Natawa was a missionary assistant and his father, Robert, had adopted Christianity. Yet Levias found it challenging to take a Christian stand. "My classmates mocked me for not following the Zuni way . . . even older folks put us down a lot."

Others spoke of the difficult choices facing them as members of this traditionally religious village and, depending on one's choices, the risk of facing criticism either from the community or from congregational members.

HOW INDIGENOUS ARE THE CHURCHES?

In most mission circles a truly indigenous church will be *self-governing, self-supporting,* and *self-multiplying.* Some add a fourth characteristic: *self-expressing.* In church circles we hear a lot about congregational health, which in part may be evaluated in relation to the same criteria. So how do Christian Navajo and Zuni leaders evaluate their vitality in light of these four "selfs"?

Self-Governing

Stanley Jim observed that small reservation churches tend to think they are healthier than others may think they are. They plan and carry out their own ministry, manage their own facilities, relate to their own communities, and strongly desire to be indigenous. As a case in point, Four Corners in Teec Nos Pos has had part-time leadership ever since Paul Redhouse retired in 1990. Yet Darlene Litson says, "We are a solid biblical preaching church. We are organized in the CRCNA, the first Native American church (on the reservation) to do so. We have graduated from Home Missions support. Our reputation is that we are a strong Navajo church." Ted Charles agrees, mostly. "For the first time the churches are able to make decisions, good or bad, for themselves. But there still is a lot of fear about doing it the right way, the way the old missionaries taught us."

A recurring concern is the shortage of trained and committed indigenous leaders. Ernest Benally of Farmington is optimistic that "no matter how difficult things are, [the people] seem to hang in there together." Yet he questions how long a church can get along well without the services of a trained leader. Dee Silver of the Tohatchi church, which also is without a pastor, agrees: "Programs and church life tend to pick up when a pastor is serving full-time." Stanley Jim shares the concern: "Every church needs to be training Native leaders. Without them we may not lose the steak, but we will lose the flavor."

Some pointed fingers at the CRC. Paul Phillips commented, "What I don't understand is why the CRC didn't do more to raise up indigenous leaders." Ernest Benally, a former mission worker himself, lamented, "Although the missionaries had good intentions, they were too insecure and did too much of the work themselves. Instead of helping assistants by training them to lead, the missionaries kept them under their control—and the transition never happened." Ed T. Begay observed on behalf of Native workers: "We got sound doctrine and catechism and so forth, but still always under the insinuation that we're not ready. Some of these folks became evangelists in other denominations. . . . I heard a radio preacher recently and said to myself, 'Other than calling people to faith, he sounds Christian Reformed to me.'"

Some pointed fingers back at themselves. One lay leader said: "Our leaders tend to hold back and, like the medicine man, expect the people to come

Edward T. Begay

to them. My idea would be for them to be more proactive, to be initiators, to start up things." Another lay leader said, "Stop saying, 'I'm available, call me.' Get something structured, offer a specific plan, and then go out and recruit!" Native pastors themselves acknowledge that it is very easy to let nonnative pastors take the leadership role. And congregational attitudes can feed into this. Ernest Benally said, "Our people are so used to seeing and having Anglos in leadership roles. . . . When a pastor leaves, the older members continue looking over the hill for another white one, all trained and paid for."

All, however, seem to agree on the solution: *more local training.* Paul Phillips notes: "[In the] long term, our being intentional needs to include more *local* training options." Ed T. Begay explains why: "For young leaders to be effective in ministry they need to know the language, and they need to pay attention to the cultural emphasis of the Navajo people. Once they have those two things in hand, they can blend it in with the Christian teachings." Stanley Jim adds, "We need to make training as local and indigenous as we can, and then bring in (Anglo) speakers as needed."

Self-Supporting

Another recurring theme is limited financial resources. Fourteen of the eighteen Red Mesa churches can be considered "reservation" churches. The majority of the fourteen are small, some very small. Several of the congregations are in very isolated communities with almost no employment opportunities. Currently, nine of the fourteen reservations churches are served by part-time or volunteer leaders. The remaining five have full-time pastors, although most, if not all, are seriously underpaid—sometimes by agreement and sometimes by default.

Classis Red Mesa in 2005

Congregation	Started*	Organized	Membership 1982	2005
Albuquerque, NM/Fellowship	1962	1978	80	110
Church Rock, NM	1950	1983	58	56+
Crownpoint, NM	1912	1971	160	139+
Farmington, NM/Maranatha	1925	1962	94	106+
Fort Wingate, NM	1930	1982	48	47+
Gallup, NM/Bethany	1928	1956	221	267
Naschitti, NM	1926	1982	83	23
Newcomb, NM	1980	-	-	?
Red Valley, AZ (formerly Red Rock)	1934	1992	213	45+
Rehoboth, NM	1903	1906	173	243
Sanostee, NM	1942	-	52	40
Shiprock, NM/Bethel	1934	1985	73	162
Teec Nos Pos, AZ/Four Corners	1934	1982	155	137
Toadlena, NM	1915	-	113	28
Tohatchi, NM/First Navajo	1898	1983	78	13
Tohlakai, NM/Bethlehem	1930	1982	128	78
Window Rock, AZ	1965	1980	113	86
Zuni, NM	1897	1987	51	264

* The start date may indicate, variously, when a location was officially adopted, a missionary established residence, or worship services were begun.

+ These membership totals are repeated from a prior year(s).

Practical solutions are elusive. Paul Phillips believes that "deep inside we Natives would like to have a church all on our own. I really don't know how that can happen on the reservation, but I think it's possible if it's done in different forms." Stanley Jim thinks a lot about how to translate that into the Navajo context. Given that CRC structures tend to be church- and location-bound, Stanley suggests we can learn from the medicine man model, which is more open. Dr. Franklin Freeland of the Gallup church said that the off-reservation churches "appear to have defiance compliance participation" toward the reservation churches and challenges them to be more generous with their professional and technical resources. Ernest Benally calls for greater unity within each congregation. "When unity happens, when there is cooperation, when the people are not fighting each other, there is a spirit of generosity. People are more ready to help each other financially, to come together and do the work together."

Ted Charles views self-support as a spiritual issue: "A church's self-sufficiency should rest on what God provides for them, no matter how large or how small. If churches view their need and what they have to fulfill that need, with a lot of prayer they can come to consensus about what way to go." Marla Jasperse said, "One of the healthiest things churches can do is to pray for one another and support and encourage each other versus each church working alone. Just like a gas station and a sandwich shop do business together, why not have a CRC church and a non-CRC church do ministry together?" Franklin Freeland calls for Navajo and Zuni pastors "to have a brainstorming session on how to overcome the issues and challenges rather than a whining session. The past is the past, and the future is the new direction for a whole new organization of indigenous pastors who know that little or no support will be coming from Grand Rapids."

Self-Multiplying

Darlene Litson says of Four Corners, "The worship is simple and accommodating, and designed to meet the needs of the present congregation" even though "sometimes we do not share the gospel; it's too much about us." Her husband James echoes her concern: "We are stuck in a rut." He too would like more emphasis on witnessing—and told of sharing the gospel when people ask him to pray for them.

Al Silver of Tohatchi likes how the members share their faith at worship services and how they invite community members to attend their yearly gospel meetings.

Edgar Bitsoie, an elderly saint from Tohatchi, said, "The worship services meet my needs when I go to church. However, we really do not allow for the youth to participate." He suspects the worship services are geared too much toward the older generation.

Paul Phillips, who is considering future ministry, is mindful of the challenge: "There are seven hundred youth out there. Some churches are doing a

The Rehoboth-Red Mesa Foundation was formed in the late 1990s as a resource arm of Classis Red Mesa and the Red Mesa Christian Schools. The foundation's major asset is eight hundred acres of land deeded to the foundation by Christian Reformed Home Missions in 2000. A primary goal of the Native American-led board is to build an endowment that will provide local assistance for the Red Mesa churches, schools, and related ministries. The foundation's goal is to begin distribution of funds in the fall of 2009. Mitzie Begay (pictured here) serves as the foundation board secretary.

few things like offering guitar lessons, but not much is going on. There's lots of potential, but people need to be ministering to those kids."

Zuni Christians spoke consistently of their desire for more Zunis to come to know Jesus. Verna Chavez said, "I am especially happy about how the body has grown lately, and that the doors are open to anybody. My prayer is that the Native people would be more open in asking questions and come to church to hear the Word of God and turn their lives around." Her cousin Virginia echoed gratitude that some new Zuni families had joined them recently. She also explained that the village is small, and that sometimes church people can discourage newcomers with gossip and in other ways. "I believe we need to learn more about welcoming others."

One person gave this example of the challenges faced by Zuni Christians: "In the Zuni language the concept of forgiveness is un-interpreted. The way you feel and what you do can be interpreted, but not forgiveness. . . . I think it is easier for the dominant society to forgive because they have words for it." Others spoke of the difficulties in deciding how to relate to traditional Zuni religious events—whether to make a total break from the Zuni culture, or whether to participate in some ways and be open to opportunities for prayer and witness. Several mentioned their excitement about the *Jesus* video that had been translated into the Zuni language and distributed throughout the pueblo. "Some people even came and asked for more copies."

Self-Expressing

Ted Charles admitted, "My parents tried to put aside cultural identity. In fact, they instructed us as Native American Christians to assimilate; they deemphasized Indian-ness. In effect I agreed with them to do that. It was after they passed on, about five years ago, that I decided to come more in contact with my culture, relearning the language, letting my hair grow, and witnessing more within the reality of my culture."

Stanley Jim believes that redeeming some traditional values would strengthen the growth of God's kingdom among the Navajo people. He notes, "For generations we developed a mindset that our traditional music was of the devil. But Reformed theology teaches that all good things come from God" (*The Banner,* September 27, 1999, pp. 14-15). A musician himself, Jim has made some attempts at using traditional-sounding music for God's glory.

Franklin Freeland urged greater appreciation for Navajo thinking: "We are a complex group of people, and hard to understand, in part because we do not explain ourselves enough. We are the 'dine'—actually a longer phrase not often quoted, the 'holy people of the land.' We are raised in a spiritual way. There is that holiness in us, around us; it's a general thing."

Ed T. Begay agreed: "I would like to see more respect for Navajo tradition. Navajos see themselves as a chosen people, and have a high regard for the sacred, readily acknowledging the Creator. . . . To communicate to our traditional people, we need to speak to the Supreme Being through

"Jesus was the greatest rodeo rider ever; he rode a colt that had never been ridden."

—Ted Charles

prayers and songs in our own language." Ed also challenged pastors to drop in at traditional ceremonies and mix with the people. "Be seen there as a Christian minister. Help build the fire, turn the fried bread. When they get to the 'communion' part say something like, 'Since I'm not fully with you, it's better for me not to take part at this point.' What it is, really, is acknowledging that the Holy Spirit will guide you."

Duane Chimoni of Zuni expressed a similar challenge: "It's good to have sound doctrine, but how do you share it in ways that reach a dyed-in-the-wool Zuni seeker? There are certain things in our culture that are redeemable, that can be used. For example, in the Zuni religion they have mentors or sponsors; perhaps we can do the same. They have a beautiful baby ceremony—the baby is shown the light of the morning, and is given a name, and the relatives come and celebrate. It's important for us to be intentional in ways that connect culturally. To be Christlike is to be what Christ wants us to be, and that's a personal thing, a cultural thing. It is important to allow the Holy Spirit to use us for the Lord."

SO WHAT'S THE PLAN?

In September 2003 Classis Red Mesa adopted a series of statements for guidance in further visioning and planning. Under the theme of "Missioned to Mission" the classis identified these priority goals:

- *Healthy congregations.* Building spiritually healthy congregations brings stability to the members, retains children and youth as they mature in their faith and life, and calls the whole church to carry out its vision for the kingdom of God.
- *The mission of God.* The various ministries in Red Mesa will work together for a common purpose in advancing the mission of God.

- *Indigenous leadership.* Our commitment to the mission and goal of raising up indigenous ministry leaders will greatly enhance growth toward spiritual maturity.
- *Unique Christian identity.* We will develop our identity and communicate our witness as Native American and Reformed Christians by identifying common cultural values that are rediscovered through the eyes of Scripture and that are deeply experienced "in Christ."
- *Biblical reconciliation.* In the process of dismantling cultural and institutional racism, we will move from "Missioned to Mission" and toward true biblical reconciliation.

—— Summarized from a Classical Home Missions Committee Report to Classis Red Mesa, September 20, 2003

Stanley Jim and his wife, Sharon

"In reconciliation, confession alone is not the end. A commitment to sustaining a lifelong changed relationship is key to living in harmony. We must leave the sins we confess at the foot of the cross. Let us not return to them. Rather, we must move forward as a forgiven people, bearing the image of Christ."

——Stanley Jim, Home Missions regional leader, Classis Red Mesa, Summer 2003

DISCUSSION STARTERS

1. For many years denominational publications referred to the Navajo and Zuni people as "Indian cousins." What do you like and/or dislike about this language?

2. Synod 1954 gave two grounds for its ultimate goal that the Navajo and Zuni churches become "fully" CRC. Discuss the relative merit of these grounds (p. 75).

3. Paul writes to the Corinthians, "Our desire is not that others might be relieved while you are hard pressed, but that there might be equality" (2 Cor. 8:13). What implications might this teaching have for building and compensation budgets of richer and poorer congregations in Red Mesa?

4. Zuni Christians speak repeatedly of their eagerness to see other Zunis come to faith. Whom are you praying will come to Jesus?

5. Discuss 1 Corinthians 9:19-23 in relation to Native leader reflections on greater sensitivity in relation to the Navajo and Zuni cultures. From a biblical perspective, what features of Navajo and Zuni culture would enrich the prevailing white culture?

CHAPTER FIVE

WE'VE COME THIS FAR BY FAITH: AFRICAN AMERICANS IN THE CRC

Reginald Smith

"Now faith is being sure of what we hope for. . . ." —Hebrews 11:1

"WHAT IS THEIR STORY?"

In the movie *Amistad*, former president John Quincy Adams' assistance is sought on behalf of the slaves aboard the ship. Not wanting to take the case, Adams offers a bit of free advice: "In the courtroom, whoever tells the best story wins." Still somewhat curious, he asks one more question of Mr. Jolsen, an ex-slave dedicated to the abolitionist cause. "What is their story, by the way?" Jolsen is taken aback. He tells Adams that the slaves are from West Africa. Adams persistently responds, "No! What is their story?" Trying to strengthen his point, he continues, "You've proven *what* they are. They are Africans. Congratulations. What you don't know and haven't bothered in the least to discover is *who* they are."

Adams knew the value of stories. The Bible values stories. Human beings value stories. Stories are the primary vehicle of explaining who we are. This is our story. Our journey. The task is not to define, but to describe some of the people, places, and social contexts that have shaped the African American journey in the Christian Reformed Church. Our story reflects the mixture of the joy and pain of being African American and Christian Reformed. Some churches are flourishing in their communities and others are floundering. Some members sing the praises of being CRC and others have left the denomination, frustrated by the slow and incremental progress of racial understanding and growth. Still others, through God's grace, work and pray and embody a fuller version of the African American contributions in the Christian Reformed Church. We will hear from some of them in this chapter.

WHAT ARE "CHAPELS" ALL ABOUT?

First impressions shape our perceptions and understandings about the people we meet. African Americans first encountered Dutch Calvinists through the doors of Christian Reformed chapels in the Midwest and on the East Coast. Buckley Chapel (now Grace CRC) in Grand Rapids; Manhattan CRC in New York; Northside Community Chapel in Paterson, New Jersey; and Pullman, Roseland, and Lawndale in Chicago were flagship stations for the entry of African Americans into the CRC.

Chapels were the first but not the only mode of outreach to African Americans. Two other approaches were used by the Christian Reformed Church: planting new churches in African American communities, and encouraging traditional congregations to transition into multiracial congregations. Since the chapels have the longer history, we will take a closer look at their overall impact.

The intent of the chapel strategy was simply to create safe space for non-Dutch folks to encounter the gospel. A side benefit was that chapels also relieved Dutch folks' uneasiness with "others" who were not familiar with CRC tradition and culture. After World War II, with the white flight to the suburbs and the relocation of new racial groups in urban areas, chapels continued as the preferred model for gaining new believers in former Dutch immigrant communities. In reality however, the chapels became the traditional CRC in a smaller package, still reflecting cultural and structural characteristics of the urban CRC in its early stages.

Early Chapels in African American Urban Areas

1914 Madison Square Chapel in Grand Rapids, Michigan; initially served white people living in poverty

1935 Baxter Street Mission in Grand Rapids, now Baxter Community Center

1949 Buckley Chapel in Grand Rapids, now Grace CRC; the first recorded intentional ministry to African Americans

1950 Evangelism was begun among African Americans in Harlem, New York City

1955 Lawndale Gospel Chapel in Chicago; began as a Jewish outreach ministry and then changed its focus to evangelizing the emerging African American community

First, most CRC chapels were headed by white lay leaders. Because CRC pastors were not often passionate about evangelism, "unordained" workers, equipped with zeal for the Reformed faith and love for people, eagerly led non-Dutch people to the saving grace of Christ. Through addressing people's physical needs and through

Upon organization in 1962, Buckley Chapel was renamed Grace CRC. Its first council (left to right): Henry Washington, Andrew Cross, Luther Ward, Martin Toonstra (pastor), William Burress

solid biblical teaching, these lay men and women worked tirelessly with and for African American people caught in the tangled web of racism, injustice, and economic hardship.

Next, these white leaders had a pipeline to CRC networks. They were the sons and daughters of the CRC. For the most part, the education they received was in CRC-related institutions. These relationships were essential for attracting human and economic resources to chapel ministries. These white leaders did not readily recognize the strength of emerging African American leadership nor easily share power with them. In fact, they often stayed put for decades, not preparing for their successors and not sufficiently helping them establish CRC networks of their own. After all, it's not what you know but who you know!

Also, the chapels were designed for ministry to the urban poor. Some folks were attracted because they had been burned in traditional African American churches. Most, however, were attracted by the charity of the white leaders. The chapels served as way stations and sanctuaries for struggling saints under the pressing conditions of urban life. In the long term, this emphasis hindered their development in two ways: first, by embracing people when they were in need, only to push them away when they were no longer in need; and second, by failing to attract middle- and upper middle-class African Americans who could have contributed much, educationally and economically, to these ministries.

Today the local and denominational climate for long-term financial support of small chapels has changed. Chapels that reached out only to people struggling to survive and that did not eventually develop into larger congregations, are themselves struggling to survive. One negative impact is that members are hampered from experiencing a more complete world-and-life-view and a culturally enriched church life. Another negative result is that if chapels are forced to close their doors, the CRC could lose many of its African American members.

Is There More to the Story?

Over the years, Baptist, Methodist, and Pentecostal churches had attracted African Americans in huge numbers. So why were not many more urban African Americans attracted to the Christian Reformed Church?

Historically, African people never went looking for white people. When African men and women caught their first glimpse of the strange shores of the American colonies, they began to sing haunting African funeral songs about their homeland. A terrible truth was sinking in: slavery would be for life. African "immigration" was not about fleeing religious persecution from their homeland; it was the capture and enslavement of

black people for economic gain. Slavery was the American holocaust, justified by religion and institutionalized by law. One of the ways these captured Africans gave voice to their pain and cultural homesickness was through song. As Israel sang their songs of lament and faith in Babylonian exile, African American people also learned to sing their songs of pain and trust in a strange land.

By God's grace something amazing happened late in the sixteenth century. In 1773, George Leile and Andrew Bryan, both former slaves, formed the first independent Baptist church in Silver Bluff, South Carolina. These pioneers, who cherished emotionally expressive worship and an independent style of church government, began a movement that attracted African Americans in droves. Restrictions and cruelties imposed by their owners, even threat of death, could not deter the independent African American church movement. The freedom to be with God and each other was the thing that kept African American folks strong and hopeful— ironically during the same time that America was trying to win its own freedom from the British throne. The African American church was the only place to be truly African American, Christian, and free!

Sheila Holmes became pastor at Northside Community Church in Paterson six years ago, on the heels of a long-time white pastor. Since that time, 35 percent of the congregation left. Of those remaining, 98 percent are low-income African Americans. Holmes is the only female pastor and only black pastor in Classis Hackensack.

The distinguishing feature of these Baptist, Methodist, and emerging Pentecostal churches was their culturally relevant worship—their worship style and music connected with African Americans' hearts. These churches ministered to their cultural homesickness. They were not perfect churches, but they "scratched where it itched." So why leave?

There's a lesson to be learned in all this. The lesson is the same for CRC chapels, for transitioning churches, and for African American church plants. Each of them is competing with these cultural and historical realities in African American church life. Any ministry that fails to offer the rich worship of the African American church will certainly bypass the wonderful opportunity to contribute to the development of a dynamic, thriving, and historically relevant African American Reformed community.

CAN CHAPELS BIRTH SCHOOLS?

One of the bright spots of the chapel model is the creation of urban Christian schools. CRC chapels gave birth to thriving urban Christian schools in the midst of three forces: failing public school systems, a commitment to Christ-centered learning, and racial reconciliation. These forces were powerful catalysts in creating educational ministries that helped to develop new African American leadership for the urban community. Here are three examples.

West Side Christian School

On Chicago's west side the nearest Christian school was Timothy Christian School—located in Cicero, the city Martin Luther King labeled the most racist city he had encountered. In the 1960s African American children were discouraged from attending Timothy, leaving the option of being bused to a much more distant Christian school in Des Plaines. In 1969, West Side Christian School was born from this crucible of racism. It began with eight African American children at Lawndale Christian Reformed Church. After thirty-five years in the African American community, West Side has added a new facility; its enrollment has soared to more than one hundred children. Western suburban churches such as Elmhurst and Cicero are now loyal partners with the school. It has a diverse teaching faculty and is growing African American leaders for the twenty-first century.

Roseland Christian School

Roseland Christian School on Chicago's near south side opened its doors in 1884. For nearly one hundred years the Roseland community had been a completely Dutch Calvinist neighborhood. But with the coming of the civil rights movement in the sixties, the racial makeup of Roseland changed "overnight." CRC people, caught up in the panic of white flight, rushed to the southern suburbs of Chicago. However, Roseland Christian School stayed and retained its mandate: to provide Christ-centered learning in the Roseland neighborhood. Today, Roseland Christian School continues to uphold this mission. With a predominantly African American student body, the school is a catalyst for new leadership and is an educational beacon of hope in the greater African American community.

Dawn Treader Christian School

The public school system in Paterson, New Jersey, was considered one of the worst in the nation. Student math and reading scores were plunging like a rock thrown into the Passaic River. Church leaders from Northside Chapel and Madison Avenue CRC dreamed of an urban Christian school housed in a former locomotive factory. In 1977, with help from some Christian businesspeople, Dawn Treader Christian School was born. A shining star with an 80 percent African American student body, Dawn Treader continues to swim against the grain of academic failure and hopelessness.

In Chicago, Paterson, and elsewhere, urban Christian education is a part of the movement of God for racial justice and equality for African Americans—and for further introducing the Christian Reformed Church as a yokefellow with African Americans.

Urban Christian School

1884
Roseland Christian School, Chicago
94 percent African American

1969
West Side Christian School, Chicago
99 percent African American

1977
Dawn Treader Christian School, Paterson, NJ
80 percent African American

WHY ARE WE HERE?

I know from personal experience that the journey for African Americans in the CRC is a lonely one. I attend many denominational meetings as the only African American in the room. I am discouraged by the negative experiences of African American leaders. I am disappointed that there are fewer than 1,000 African American members in the CRC. I am frustrated by the single-digit total of African American graduates from Calvin Theological Seminary, and the small number of African American church plants since 1970.

At the same time, I am thankful for the pastors and leaders who have gone ahead of me. I stand proudly on their shoulders today. Let's meet two courageous and patient African American men who are an integral part of CRC history.

Eugene St. Clair Callender, pioneer African American pastor in the CRC

Eugene Callender

Eugene St. Clair Callender graduated from Boston University in 1947, the same year Jackie Robinson broke the color line in baseball's major league. Four years later, Callender became the first African American pastor in the CRC. Being the first Black of anything is never easy, including the first African American pastor in the CRC. But unlike Robinson's carefully orchestrated entrance into major league baseball, Callender is convinced his entrance into the CRC was designed and orchestrated directly by God.

Callender was from the Boston area, a product of the African American Pentecostal church. He felt drawn to ministry and applied to well-known seminaries like Harvard and Yale, but with no response. He had been an InterVarsity student leader at his university, and two days before graduation an InterVarsity staff member suggested he consider Westminster Seminary in Philadelphia. When Callender received their catalogue, what impressed him was that they did not ask applicants to indicate their race. He applied and was accepted.

As Callender tells the story, "I entered the seminary lobby and was approached by a colored gentleman who was vacuuming. I asked him to direct me to the registrar's office, but he dropped the vacuum and ran. A moment later he came back with the secretary, Margaret Robinson. I told her who I was and why I was there. Shocked, she also ran! Pretty soon a stately white gentleman approached me and introduced himself as Paul Wooley, professor of church history and the school registrar." When Callender asked what was going on, Wooley acknowledged they were surprised that he was 'colored.' Callender explained that the application form did not ask about race, and he assumed this was a liberal seminary where race did not matter. Wooley was quick to point out that Westminister was not liberal, and that they probably had not asked about race because "they never had (a black student), and never thought they'd get one." At the same time, Wooley assured Callender he was welcome. And by Callender's own testimony, Westminster proved to be a great experience. He was introduced to Reformed thinking and attracted to it. He also served as class president and president of the student body.

Now for the CRC connection! Who should speak at Callender's graduation but Rev. Peter Eldersveld, radio minister of the church's "Back to God Hour." Eldersveld was aware that the radio broadcast ministry's New York City audience included many African Americans. In God's providence Eldersveld met Callender after the graduation ceremony and asked him what he planned to do. Callender said he didn't know, so Eldersveld hired him on the spot— to follow up on radio response among African Americans in New York City. Around this same time the Back to God Hour hired pastor Harold Dekker of Englewood (N.J.) CRC as assistant radio minister. It was Dekker who first urged Callender to consider becoming an ordained minister in the CRC. Dekker recruited the support of pastor Nick Monsma of Second Paterson, perhaps the most conservative church in the classis—thinking if they would buy it, so would classis. Dekker also helped win the support of

Home Missions director Harry Blystra for starting a church among African Americans in New York City. On September 12, 1951, Callender was ordained and installed as a minister of the Word in the CRC. This is the first record of intentional denominational CRC ministry to African Americans.

Harlem, the first settlement of Dutch Calvinists in America, had become the home of African American life in New York City. And Harlem became Callender's base of operation for bringing the Reformed faith to a place that had become very different from that early Dutch settlement. He started out in a storefront, but no one would come for worship. So he conducted outdoor worship services from one street to another. Over time God honored Callendar's boldness with many African Americans coming to faith in Jesus Christ, and with many CRC leaders and members supporting his ministry. In 1952 the ministry purchased a five-story "storefront" on the corner of Seventh Avenue and 122nd Street and transformed the first two floors into a worship and ministry center. In the years following, Callender worked hard and prayed hard to present a relevant Reformed faith that fit the challenging social and cultural conditions of African Americans in Harlem.

The new work in Manhattan flourished, as did Callender's holistic word and deed philosophy of ministry. However, his practice of wearing a clerical collar, coupled with a strong leadership style and "activist" sympathies, led to suspicion of Callender's theology among some denominational leaders. Callender observed, "There is a strong element of suspicion about me and my aims in Harlem. This may stem from the usual suspicion "outsiders" generally receive from the CRC, or it may be that there are basic cultural differences that can never be resolved" ("First Black CRC Minister Returns to Church's Pulpit," *Grand Rapids Press,* April 21, 2001). With these words Callender put his finger on a frustration often felt by African American pastors providing leadership in the CRC even today.

In 1959, in the face of questions about his future in the CRC because of marital difficulties (and knowing a divorced minister would not have been tolerated by the CRC in that era), Callender accepted the pastorate of a large Presbyterian Church (USA) a few blocks away. In the course of his distinguished ministry Dr. Callender also began a prep school in Harlem and advised five presidents—but he did not return to a CRC pulpit for forty-two years.

The ice was broken in 2001 when he accepted an invitation to preach at Immanuel CRC in Kalamazoo. At that time he referred to his earlier departure as a blessing in disguise: "I am deeply grateful to the Christian Reformed Church for helping give birth to my ministry. I still believe the CRC has a powerful theology. It has a solid message that the world needs to hear." At its 2002 multi-ethnic conference, then general secretary David Engelhard, in a reciprocal spirit, spoke the CRC's appreciation to Callender: "We honor him as a pioneer leader who served Christ and the CRC among African Americans."

Emmett Harrison

Let's meet a younger pioneer, the Reverend Emmett Harrison. Growing up in Meridian, Mississippi, during the 1950s, the African American church and community were his refuge, providing safety, comfort, and stability. Pastor Samuel Williams, the first person in Harrison's community to get a tape recorder, used it to record Harrison and other children singing gospel songs. Williams became Harrison's role model.

Harrison's world was turned upside down by a move to Chicago in 1961. Living on the south side along Ashland Avenue (the racial divider between African Americans and white people) Harrison was introduced to northern racism. He was among the first African American students to integrate a local white high school. Excelling in football and band, and functioning with relative ease in the two worlds, he became a bridge-builder between the races.

Rev. Emmett Harrison,
first African American officer
of the CRC synod

In 1973, shortly after Harrison entered Chicago State University, two young African Americans—Fred Hampton and Mark Clark—were gunned down by Chicago police officers. They were suspected Black Panthers, and they were unarmed. Their deaths plunged Harrison into a deep hole of despair. African Americans did not seem to be worth much in America.

The silence of the church nagged at Harrison. Its prophetic voice for social justice and civil rights seemed mute and impotent. By contrast, the Panthers had a progressive social agenda and vocal love for black people. In his despair he joined the Panthers. Maybe, he thought, being a martyr could bring about justice and equality.

God revealed another option. Emmett's point of despair became a point of hope. The Clark and Hampton deaths prompted him to fight racism and oppression from within the system. God first opened doors in the corporate world, where Harrison honed his organizational skills. At the same time, God placed on Harrison's heart a call to pastoral ministry. While Harrison and his wife Emily were raising their small children, he sold insurance during the day and searched for a ministry opportunity at night. In 1981, Harrison encountered Rev. Tony Van Zanten, pastor of Roseland Christian Ministry Center. When Van Zanten told Harrison that the Christian Reformed Church was interested in bringing African American leaders into pastoral ministry, Harrison sensed God's confirmation of his call.

Harrison was ordained in 1987 and became assistant pastor and head of men's ministries at Roseland. There he came to appreciate the Reformed approach to holistic ministry: "Reformed theology became a way of transforming the world. I love the Reformed worldview. . . . It must become real, and the church must make it real." In 1990 Harrison accepted a pastorate at East Side CRC in suburban Cleveland, Ohio. There he used his bridge-building and organizational skills to transition a mostly white church into a multiracial congregation.

As a senior pastor and member of classis, he gained increased access to the organizational system in the CRC. For six years he served on the board of Christian Reformed Home Missions, his concluding years as vice president. In June 2004 he made CRC history as the first African American to serve as an officer of synod, the CRC's broadest assembly. Harrison said, "[My election] does represent a continual step toward opening up and being more inclusive" ("CRC Synod Elects First Black Officer," *Grand Rapids Press*, June 13, 2004). From the fields of Mississippi to the streets of Chicago to the suburbs of Cleveland, God uses our twists and turns for his purposes and plans.

HOW DO BLACKS GET CREDENTIALED IN A WHITE SYSTEM?

The first four African American pastors— Callender, Virgil Patterson, James White and Rick Williams—came to the CRC with both ministry experience and seminary training. More often than not, this experience and training occurred outside the CRC, but it did occur and was recognized. This suggests that an educated clergy is a clear value for African American congregations as well as for the CRC in general.

African American* Pastors Serving in the CRC

Began	Name	Position
1981	Rick Williams	Pullman CRC, Chicago, IL
1981	Dante Venegas	Madison Square and City Hope, Grand Rapids, MI; now emeritus
1981	D.A. Crushshon	Back to God CRC, Chicago, IL
1982	Don Sherow	Grace, Grand Rapids, MI, Madison Ave, Paterson, NJ, church plant in Chesapeake, VA; eligible for call
1985	Emmett Harrison	Roseland CRC, Chicago, IL and East Side CRC, Cleveland, OH
1993	Reginald Smith	Northside, Paterson, NJ and Roosevelt Park, Grand Rapids, MI
1995	Robert Price	Home Missions Regional Leader, based in Chicago, IL
1997	Jerome Burton	Coit Community, Grand Rapids, MI
1997	George Boyd	Vision One church plant, Atlanta, GA
1998	Sheila Holmes	Northside Community, Paterson, NJ
1998	Timothy Blackmon	River Rock CRC plant, Folsom, CA
1999	Denise Posie	Immanuel CRC, Kalamazoo, MI
2000	Ron Black	New Ground Harvest plant, Los Angeles, CA
2000	George Cooper	Fox Valley CRC, Crystal Lake, IL
2001	George Davis, Jr.	Oakdale Park CRC, Grand Rapids, MI
2001	Jeffery Hough	Angel Community Church, Muskegon, MI
2002	Melvin Jackson	Grace Unlimited plant, Los Angeles, CA
2004	Lawrence Bennett	Gardena Community plant, Los Angeles, CA
2004	Robert Stevenson	City Hope Ministries, Grand Rapids, MI
2005	Joseph Wright	King's Chapel Harvest plant, Los Angeles, CA
2005	Angela Taylor Perry	Church of the Servant, Grand Rapids, MI

*This list includes Venegas and Williams, of Puerto Rican and Panamanian descent respectively, who came alongside and identified for decades with the African American CRC experience. The list does not include pastors who emigrated from Africa, some of whom also increasingly identify with the African American experience. We apologize for the omission of any who should have been named but were not.

Beginning in the 1980s, with the growing demand for African American leadership, classes also began approving ordination on the basis of "extraordinary gifts" and ordination to the office of ministry associate—in both instances without all the prescribed training. At the same time, the pattern of receiving seminary trained African American clergy from other denominations continues. Simultaneously, the last decade has enjoyed an increase in African American leaders in training at Calvin Seminary.

We still have a long way to go in raising up more home grown leadership in the CRC. And we need to remain flexible as the Lord provides leadership among us. May God continue to nurture among us a love for learning and an African American "feel" in the mentoring of new leaders.

African American Pastoral Leaders Who Left the CRC

Began	Name	Position	Status
1951	Eugene Callender	Manhattan CRC, NYC	Left CRC in 1959
1969	James White	Manhattan CRC, NYC	Left Manhattan in 1971, and the ministry in 1975
1973	Virgil Patterson	Fuller Ave and Madison Square, Grand Rapids, MI	Left in 1977, now deceased
1982	Rodney Alexander	First CRC, Grand Rapids, MI	Left in 1988
1984	John Nash	Grace, Grand Rapids, MI and Christ Community plant, Atlanta, GA	Christ Community closed in 2001, now teaches at a Bible college
1987	Victor Anderson	Grace CRC, Grand Rapids, MI	Seminary professor in TN
1991	Sam Murrell	Indian Harbour Beach CRC, FL	Left CRC ministry in 1992
1993	Greg Cumberland	Madison Square CRC, Grand Rapids, MI	Left CRC ministry in 1995
1995	Rayfield Benton	Oakdale CRC, Grand Rapids, MI	Left CRC ministry in 2000
1996	Glandion Carney	CentrePointe CRC, Grand Rapids, MI	Left CRC ministry in 1997
1998	Eric Gray	Maple Ave CRC, Holland, MI	Left CRC ministry in 2004
1998	Andre Daley*	CentrePointe CRC, Grand Rapids, MI	Left in 2002, now at RCA plant

*Andre Daley is from Jamaica but identifies with the African American experience.

WHERE DO WE STAND?

African American leaders face many ongoing struggles within the predominantly white—and often culturally separate—Christian Reformed settings. Rev. Robert Price, African American coordinator for Christian Reformed Home Missions remarked, "African Americans come into the [CRC] denomination through the 'front door' of theology, only to exit the 'back door' for cultural reasons" ("Understanding the Dutch-American Christian Reformed Subculture and Tradition," In-Ministry paper, Northern Baptist Theological Seminary, Aug. 1, 1994). Some African Americans (including Eugene Callender) left the CRC feeling it did not allow a full-orbed expression of African American spirituality.

Others, like Harrison, are determined to continue negotiating the still dominant Dutch-American landscape, working and praying for greater inclusion in the CRC and more complete unity under Christ as Lord.

Various "Firsts" for African Americans in the CRC

Started	Name	Organization and Position
1970	Reuben Smartt	Calvin College, Upward-Bound Program
1981	James White	Calvin College. Sociology department
1984	Terri Harris	Calvin College, Director of Multicultural Affairs
1987	Victor Anderson	Received Master of Divinity degree from Calvin Seminary
1988	Ruth Buntin	CRWRC, Serving Learning Coordinator
1988	Yvonne Rayburn-Beckley	CRCNA Ministry of Race Relations, regional leader
1990	Al Brewton	CRCNA, Director of CRC Biennial Multiethnic Conference
1991	James White	CR Home Missions, African American Ministries Coordinator
1993	Norma Coleman	CRCNA Ministries, Director of Human Resources
1994	Lyman Howell	CRWRC, Regional Consultant
1994	Earl James	Madison Square Church, Director of Ministries and Communication
2000	Victoria Gibbs	CR Home Missions, Small Group Ministry Developer
2000	Jennifer Parker	CRC Publications, staff writer, *The Banner*
2003	Melissa James	CR Home Missions, Financial Officer
2004	Emmett Harrison	CRCNA, Vice President of Synod
2005	Laura Carpenter	Madison Square Church, Director of Diversity and Certified CRCNA Anti-Racism Trainer
2005	Denise Stevenson	CR Home Missions, Church Planting and Development leader
2005	Angela Taylor Perry	Master of Divinity, Calvin Seminary

Bultman Studios Inc.

Denise Stevenson, Home Missions Church Planting and Development leader

The struggle to recruit and maintain an African American CRC community calls for our best efforts because the stakes are high! People such as James White and Robert Price were appointed by Christian Reformed Home Missions to nurture and encourage African American leadership and churches. The Urban Mission Board stimulated financial resources and held the denomination's feet to the fire about the concerns of African Americans. The Black and Reformed Leadership Association explored partnerships with black and Reformed communities in other denominations with significant African American memberships, and created learning networks for emerging pastoral and lay leaders. Some of these efforts succeeded and some never got off the starting block, but all helped us find a safe place to be ourselves fully and helped stop the pastoral leadership drain. We have learned much from the mistakes of the past. Let's not repeat them. By building on the foundation laid by early leaders, we have an opportunity to create a thriving community that is both fully African American and fully Reformed.

The story of African Americans in the Christian Reformed Church is ongoing. Most of the religious people in Jesus' day were mad at Jesus because he insisted on being who he was: fully human and fully God. The tension of all African Americans in the CRC is to be fully black and fully Reformed. When we acknowledge this tension, we can begin to walk with maturity and with the hope that African Americans in the CRC will help the denomination to become a house of prayer for all people. As African Americans in the CRC, our creed is this: We've come this far by faith!

DISCUSSION STARTERS

1. Reflect on the *Amistad* story. Why is it important for CRC members to hear the story of African Americans in the CRC?

2. What are the strengths and weaknesses of the chapel model? What kind of church would attract African Americans to the CRC today?

3. Why did many African American leaders leave the CRC? How can the CRC recruit and retain African American leaders in the twenty-first century?

4. What can we learn from the stories of Eugene Callender and Emmett Harrison?

5. Reflect on Robert Price's comment: "African Americans come to the CRC denomination through the 'front door' of theology, only to exit through the 'back door' for cultural reasons." Do you agree or disagree, and why?

CHAPTER SIX

Y EL CIRCULO SIGUE CRECIENDO (AND THE CIRCLE KEEPS GROWING)

Manny Bersach

"The kingdom of heaven is like a mustard seed. . . ." —Matthew 13:31

The stories in this chapter are drawn from a people group who made their way to North America from Europe mostly by way of South America, Central America, and the Caribbean Islands.

These neighbors from the south are a combination of indigenous "Indians" (as they were called) together with the Spaniards and Italians who "discovered" the new lands. As I came to realize during the time I lived in Chile as a missionary, Italians, Spaniards, Germans, and others left their "fingerprints" not only on *Latin* America but on every country in the Americas.

In places like Cuba, the indigenous people did not thrive under these changes and the labor forced on them. In fact, their numbers were diminished. So in Cuba, as in the United States, people from Africa were brought in to provide cheap labor. Over time, the features of the indigenous people became less pronounced and African features became more prominent in the greater Cuban population. This also is true of the population in other islands such as Puerto Rico and the Dominican Republic.

WHO ARE HISPANICS IN THE UNITED STATES?

Hispanic is a term popularized by the United States census bureau to include historically Spanish-speaking persons also self-identified as Chicanos, Latin Americans, Latino/Latinas, or by their country of origin. I use the term *Hispanic* intentionally because it is the preference of those I conferred with from our people group.

The presence of Hispanics in the United States dates back hundreds of years. Of the more than 40 million Hispanics in the United States today, more than 22 million—55 percent—are second-, third-, fourth-generation (and higher) American born. (All of the Spanish-sounding names in California and Texas were not selected from a Spanish dictionary!) However, throughout the United States, and especially in places like Florida, there was a major influx of Hispanic people in the 1950s and 1960s. Since then, massive Hispanic immigration also has occurred in California and Texas and elsewhere. The following information, based primarily on 2000 census data, helps paint a more complete picture.

Hispanics in the U.S. by Country of Origin

Mexican	63%
Puerto Rican	10%
Cuban	4%
Dominican Republic	3%
Salvadoran	3%
Other Central American	4%
South American	4%
Other Latino nationalities	8%

——PEW HISPANIC CENTER TABULATIONS FROM THE 2000 CENSUS

The United States is the third-largest Hispanic country in the world, with 40.5 million Hispanics. Hispanics now total 14 percent of the population in the U.S., making them the largest numerical minority ethnic/cultural group in the country. And that's not counting those who crossed the Mexican border last night. There are literally millions of "illegal aliens" in the U.S. In addition, nearly 5 million Hispanics are dual citizens of Puerto Rico and the United States.

The median age of all Hispanic persons in the U.S. is 26 years. Fifty-seven percent of Hispanics have completed a high school education. The median annual household income is around $40,000, with one-third earning over $50,000. In the United States the Hispanic population is increasing at a rate of 9 percent annually compared to the national rate of 6 percent annually.

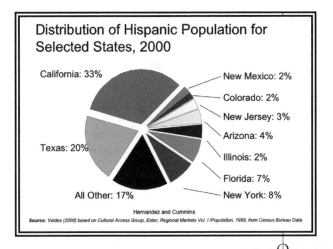

Distribution of Hispanic Population for Selected States, 2000

California: 33%
New Mexico: 2%
Colorado: 2%
New Jersey: 3%
Arizona: 4%
Illinois: 2%
Texas: 20%
Florida: 7%
All Other: 17%
New York: 8%

Hernandez and Cummins

Source: Valdes (2000) based on Cultural Access Group, Exter, Regional Markets Vol. I /Population, 1999, from Census Bureau Data

A brief analysis of the above distribution reveals some interesting facts: 83 percent of U.S. Hispanics live in nine states, 50 percent of U.S. Hispanics live in California and Texas. It's also important to note that 21 percent of all Hispanics are concentrated in Los Angeles, New York, and Miami; the states with the fastest growth in Hispanic population are North Carolina, Tennessee, Arkansas, Georgia, and South Carolina. By 2010 the Hispanic population in the United States is projected to have increased to 50 million.

Market research has uncovered attitudes toward the use of the Spanish language that churches will do well to observe. Of all Hispanic persons in the U.S., 85 percent speak Spanish in their homes, 80 percent prefer speaking in Spanish, and 52 percent prefer speaking Spanish in every situation. Interestingly, 69 percent believe that the Spanish language is more important to them today than it was five years ago.

Distribution of Hispanic Population for Selected States, 2000 Census
----HERNANDEZ AND CUMMINS, VALDES (2000) BASED ON CULTURAL ACCESS GROUP, EXTER, REGIONAL MARKETS VOL I/POPULATION, 1999, FROM CENSUS BUREAU DATA

SE HABLA ESPAÑOL

What About Hispanics in the Christian Reformed Church?

A Denominational Overview

Ministry in the CRC among Spanish-speaking people began as early as the 1940s in Chicago, New Jersey, and West Michigan, and in the 1960s in Florida and California. Initially most of those ministering in Spanish were of Dutch origin and had learned Spanish as a second language—men like Jerry Pott, Clarence Nyenhuis, and Fred Diemer. The first indigenous Hispanic leaders, Carlos Cortina and Carlos Tapia-Ruano, arose in the 1960s, and in the providence of God they were followed by a great train of CRC leaders of Hispanic origin.

Dr. Gary Teja, former Hispanic Ministry and Southeast U.S. Team Leader, Home Missions

Mrs. Viviana Cornejo, Small Group Ministry Developer and Assistant to Dr. Teja

At this writing there are thirty CRC Hispanic congregations in the United States and a growing number of related Hispanic ministries. About two-thirds of these churches are officially organized CRC congregations, with the other one-third in various stages of development. There also are a number of Hispanic outreach programs among predominantly white congregations that may result in a multiethnic congregation or a new Hispanic congregation. The thirty Hispanic congregations report a combined total of 1,500 members, for a below-average size of about fifty members per congregation.

Children and youth appear to make up only 35 percent of the total CRC Hispanic members reported, a pattern that is in contrast to Hispanic population trends in general. One possibility to account for this may be that many Hispanic youth may choose to participate in English-language ministries, and that as they marry and have children, they are bitten by the cultural bug, and Spanish becomes more important to them again. Dr. Gary Teja and Mrs. Viviana Cornejo of CRC Home Missions, who assisted with this statistical overview, also reported that they were aware of seven Hispanic persons currently in the employ of CRC denominational agencies.

Name of CRC Church/Ministry	Start Date*	Pastor/Leader
Bayamón, PR/Príncipe de Paz	2003	Hector Orlandi
Bayonne, NJ/El Regalo de Dios	2000	Roberto D. Cálix
Clifton, NJ/Nuevo Horizonte	2001	Marco A. Avila
**Greater New Jersey/Adelante Training	2000	Ramón Orostizaga
Hialeah, FL/Comunidad de Cristo	1999	Gianni Gracia
Jersey City, NJ/Jersey City Mission	1990	Ramón Orostizaga
Miami, FL/El Buen Samaritano	1964	Pedro Toledo
Miami, FL/Iglesia Buenas Nuevas	1992	Xavier Suárez
Miami, FL/Iglesia Piedras Vivas	2001	Manuel Bersach
Miami, FL/Iglesia Renacer	2001	Hector Garcia
Miami, FL/Vida Nueva	2003	Juan Pablo Sánchez
Paterson, NJ/Jesús te llama	1997	Guillermo Godoy
**Paterson, NJ/Passaic County Community College	2000	Hernán Zapata
Prospect Park, NJ/El Buen Pastor	1975	Ricardo E. Orellana
Queens, NY/Iglesia Gracia	2002	Arturo Olguin

*The start date may be when ministry began or when the church was "organized" as a CRC congregation. In the case of Puerto Rico, 2003 marks the date of affiliation with classis Southeast USA.

**These ministries are not a separate congregation but a church-related ministry, whether for congregational or educational outreach, leadership training, or coordination/consultation.

Eastern/Southeastern United States

The Hispanic population may differ significantly by national origin from one area of the United States to another. As a case in point, Puerto Ricans are more concentrated in northeastern states such as New Jersey and New York. By contrast, in predominantly Hispanic Miami and Dade County, two out of every three persons are Hispanic, and six out of every ten Hispanics have Cuban roots. Although Hispanics generally are diverse racially as well as ethnically, many white persons of Cuban origin have chosen to assimilate into the dominant white culture.

Name of CRC Church/Ministry	Start Date	Pastor/Leader
Chicago, IL/GAP Community	2001	John Zayas
Chicago, IL/Grace and Peace	1985	Pedro Avilas
Grand Rapids, MI/Iglesia Paz Y Esperanza	2002	Mario Matos (student)
*Grand Rapids, MI/Roosevelt Park Hispanic	2004	Pablo Canché
*Palos Heights, IL/La Hora de la Reforma	1965	Guillermo Serrano
Holland, MI/Mision Rey de Reyes	1997	Florencio López
Holland, MI/Nida Nueva	1964	Enrique Gomez
*Sioux Center, IA/Amistad	2003	Arturo Gomez
Wyoming, MI/Emanuel	1972	Carlos Tápanes

*These ministries are not a separate congregation but a church-related ministry, whether for congregational or educational outreach, leadership training, or coordination/consultation.

Central United States

As elsewhere, in the U.S. midsection there is great diversity among Hispanics in terms of national origin. Initial concentrations of Puerto Ricans in Chicago and Cuban immigrants in Grand Rapids were joined by Mexican nationals—now in most U.S. communities—usually sprinkled generously throughout with Hispanics who migrated from Central and South American countries.

Southern and Western United States

As in Florida and West Michigan, the CRC began intentional outreach to Cuban refugees in California in the 1960s. This outreach expanded quickly to embrace other Hispanic population groups. Some Hispanic immigrants are determined to function in multiracial and multicultural congregational settings. However, the majority of first-generation Hispanics are attracted to Spanish-speaking congregations. In several instances throughout the CRC, the people in one Hispanic congregation may hail from a dozen different countries. In the west and southwest, Hispanics emigrated primarily from Mexico, followed by large migrations from Central and South America.

Ms. Mirtha M. Villafañe R. has served as CRC Hispanic Ministry Developer since 2002, recruiting and helping train Hispanic church planters to lead Hispanic and multiethnic churches in southern California.

Name of CRC Church/Ministry	Start Date	Pastor/Leader
Anaheim, CA/Latin American	1969	Francisco Golón
*Bellflower, CA/Rosewood Hispanic Ministry	2004	Samuel Flores
*Chandler, AZ/Hispanic Outreach	2004	Cimelitza Escalona
Long Beach, CA/Nueva Comunidad	1998	Orlando Alfaro
Mount Vernon, WA/Vida Nueva	2000	Joe Strong
Pasadena, CA/GateWay CRC	2003	Daniel Mendez
Pomona, CA/Bethesda Hispanic	1997	Albino Melendez
San Diego, CA/Monte Sión	2002	(vacant—recruiting)
Simi Valley, CA/Remanente	2005	Hector Chavez
Socorro, TX/Valley Ridge Community	2002	José Rayas
Sun Valley, CA/Sol del Valle	1981	(vacant—recruiting)
Sunnyside, WA/Iglesia Evangelica	1999	Gerry Muller
Yucaipa, CA/Santa Ana Church Plant	2005	John Gonzalez
*West Coast *Adelante* Training	2000	Albino Melendez
*West Coast Hispanic Ministry Developer	2002	Mirtha Villafañe

*These ministries are not a separate congregation but a church-related ministry, whether for congregational or educational outreach, leadership training, or coordination/consultation.

WHAT PROPELS THIS MASSIVE MIGRATION TO THE NORTH?

Several significant factors contributed to Hispanic expansion northward. The first was "The Bracero Agreement" of 1942-1943. This agreement, adopted by Mexico and the United States, allowed Mexican citizens to do agricultural work in the United States. Many people of Mexican origin had remained in Arizona, California, Colorado, Nevada, and New Mexico after their lands were taken over by the United States following the War with Mexico in 1845-1848. The flow of migrant workers after 1942 joined forces with original Mexican settlers who had been living in the Southwestern United States for centuries.

A second major contributing factor to the recent influx of Hispanics into the United States has been the political instability of countries in Latin America. Some notable examples are the national revolutions of the 1970s and 1980s in Central America in places such as El Salvador, Guatemala, and Nicaragua. For similar reasons, there were large migrations to the United States from several countries in South America.

A third factor is the sheer economic hardship of millions of people in Mexico and countries further south, coupled with the opportunities for work—even if under minimal conditions—in the U.S. Some observers have said that, based on the sustained pace of legal and illegal immigration in recent decades, Mexico may have lost the battle but will yet win the war!

CONVERSATIONS WITH CRC HISPANIC PASTORS

The First Cuban Wave

Pastor Ramón Borrego started his ministry in Cuba after graduating from seminary there in the mid 1950s. Initially Borrego was influenced by the CRC through the work of missionaries Clarence

Nyenhuis and Vicente Izquierdo; he began ministering with the CRC in the Cuban city of Matanzas. He and his wife, Norma, left communist Cuba in 1966 by way of Spain. Their journey brought them to Grand Rapids, and on to ministry in Hoboken, New Jersey. In 1972 they began serving as CRC missionaries in Argentina.

Pastor Ramón Borrego and his wife, Norma

In 1978 Pastor Borrego responded to God's call to serve a new mission field within the geographical borders of the United States in what came to be known as "the gateway to Latin America"—Miami, Florida. Pastor Borrego became the first Hispanic pastor of *El Buen Samaritano* (Good Samaritan), a work started under Rev. Clarence Nyenhuis in response to the first Cuban exodus in 1960. Borrego's first two years at *El Buen Samaritano* focused on the folks who had fled Cuba twenty years earlier. In 1980 the work expanded to enfold a second major wave of Cubans—the *Marielitos,* so named because they left Cuba from the Port of Mariel.

El Buen Samaritano grew and prospered under Borrego's leadership, leading to a partnership with CRC Home Missions in birthing a daughter church in 1985—*El Redentor* (Redeemer) in nearby Hialeah. With his mission heart still beating strong, in 1989 Borrego accepted yet another ministry challenge—as founding pastor of a new Hispanic church in Miami, *Buenas Nuevas* (Good News).

Since his "retirement" in 1995, Borrego continues to be active in *Buenas Nuevas,* in assisting other Hispanic churches, and in serving on the area Hispanic task force. In a recent task force meeting, Borrego reflected on his experiences as a CRC Hispanic leader, saying, "the laying down of new trails was not easy." Having come from Cuba, his ministerial credentials were questioned and his classical (re)exam was quite thorough. Borrego, together with others like Josué Abreu and Domingo Romero, blazed new trails for others to follow and expand.

A unique challenge at *El Buen Samaritano* was pastoring a people who planned on returning to Cuba as soon as possible. Families divided by only ninety miles of water longed for political changes that would allow them to return home. History would tell another story: just twenty years after the first exodus there was a second major exodus with no return plan in sight. In the providence of God, Borrego was a leading force in the development of *El Buen Samaritano, El Redentor* and *Buenas Nuevas*—the three churches that were foundational to expanding CRC Hispanic ministry in South Florida.

The Second Cuban Wave
God is good! One person from "the second Cuban wave" whose life God touched was a young man by the name of Juan Pablo (John Peter) Sánchez. Pastor Sánchez was a product of both *El Buen Samaritano* and *El Redentor.* He and his wife, Alicia, were willing to pay the price to answer God's call to ministry. They moved to Grand Rapids for study at Calvin Seminary, only to find that English became a barrier to doing seminary-level course work. Still convinced of God's call to ministry, he was mentored and trained by his pastor, the Rev. Marcelo Sánchez (no relation), and pursued further preparation through the Florida chapter of the *Adelante* program and

through the South Florida Center for Theological Studies. Throughout this time he also continued to train as a pastoral leader by way of serving full-time in assistant ministry roles.

Pastor Juan Pablo Sánchez, his wife, Alicia, and family

Finally, in 2001, Sánchez was called to plant a new church, Vida Nueva (New Life), in the greater Miami area. We have seen God's hand on this man, his family, and his work. Although the church does not have a permanent facility and has had to move more than once, God has added greatly to their numbers, especially through the use of small group ministries. In these first four years God has blessed their sacrifice with the fastest-growing and largest of our Miami churches.

From Costa Rica to California

Pastor Gilbert Varela was born in Costa Rica in an urban area near the capital city of San José. He was reared as a nominal Roman Catholic. At the age of seventeen Varela "met the Lord" through the ministry of a conservative Christian church. Soon after becoming a Christian, he left for Mexico to study medicine. Although he had felt all along that God was calling him to ministry, it was in Mexico City that he finally answered God's call, enrolling at the Presbyterian Theological Seminary to prepare for becoming a pastor. During his last year there, one of his professors gave him a letter from Calvin Theological Seminary, which challenged students to consider advanced theological studies. He decided to accept the challenge. After completing a Master of Theology program at Calvin, Varela served in Costa Rica for two years, and then in Mexico for two years.

In 1994 the Lord again brought him into relationship with the CRC when Sun Valley (California) CRC called him to become their pastor. During the next eleven years God used Pastor Varela to lead the growing Sol del Valle congregation and to plant other churches. By Varela's own testimony, the thing that has kept him within the CRC is its "deepest respect for the Scripture and Reformed doctrine, and the spirit of inclusiveness among us."

As Varela looks to the twenty-first century, he is keenly aware of various challenges facing Hispanic churches. Many of them are in urgent need of trained leadership and improved facilities. At the same time, he urges congregations and classes to recognize and affirm Hispanic pastors for their gifts without discrimination based on educational achievements. "The fact that I went to Calvin doesn't make me better than others who may have gone to Bible institutes." Finally, he stresses the importance of empowering Hispanic leaders in the ministry and outreach of predominantly non-Hispanic congregations. "Look for opportunities to put more color in the mix!"

From Nicaragua to Washington
Pastor Gerry Muller was born in Bilwaskarma Rió Coco, Nicaragua, among a mixture of cultures and ethnicities and a diversity of races. The village of his birth continues to speak the Miskito dialect today. His first exposure to Christianity was through a nearby Moravian Mission, and later with the *Evangelical Faculty of Studies of Theology* (FEET in Spanish), a project of the Nicaraguan government that advanced liberation theology.

With his country in political turmoil, Muller came to the United States in 1986. Four years later he began training with the CRC-sponsored *Adelante* training program. He also joined the staff of the CRC church plant in El Monte,

California—both led by Pastor Gary Schipper. In 1992 Muller was ordained as an evangelist for continuing service with the El Monte ministry. He also gained broader understanding of CRC Hispanic ministry through serving on the area Hispanic Task Force and the national Hispanic Planning Team.

Pastor Gerry Muller

The Mullers moved to Sunnyside, Washington, in 1998 to head up a pioneer ministry among Hispanics in the Yakima Valley. They were warmly received by Sunnyside CRC, a large, traditional, and predominantly Dutch-American congregation. One surprise was the diversity of the Hispanic community here: undocumented first-generation migrant workers, first-generation workers with agriculture and the dairy industry, and "educated" second- and third-generation Hispanics in "white collar" jobs.

Today that ministry, called Evangelical CRC of Sunnyside, is an almost financially independent bilingual (Spanish and English) ministry with two pastors and a large diaconal ministry. Evangelical CRC also has launched an *Adelante* program with a view to training leaders for planting new Hispanic CRC churches throughout the state of Washington.

From Chicago to Chicago

Pastor Johnny Zayas is a second-generation Hispanic. His parents were from Puerto Rico and made their way to the United States in the late 1950s. Johnny was born in Chicago, grew up in a very Anglo context, and was touched by God at a youth camp at age twelve.

Some years later Johnny met up with a certain Edwin Caraballo during a softball game. This was the beginning of God separating for himself a young Hispanic leader who would reach out among people of Puerto Rican and Mexican origin in the Chicago area. Caraballo invited Johnny to attend a home Bible study on the subject of Christian marriage. The rest of the story is being written now as Johnny, with his wife, Angelina, and their family, is engaged in church-planting ministry.

Having developed as an effective Christian leader in the Young Life movement, and with the encouragement of pastor Pedro Aviles of Grace and Peace Church in urban Chicago, Zayas started the groundwork for a church plant that was subsequently named GAP Community (named after Grace and Peace, and for "standing in the gap"). Pastor Zayas led GAP's first worship service in September 2002, and has reached out into the community with Coffeehouse, Harvest Fest, and a variety of Bible studies.

Zayas acknowledged that he has run into stereotypes: "You are uneducated," "You are limited in your abilities," and the like. But he also is comfortable in the environment where he serves, and is grateful for special people who took a young Puerto Rican kid, invested in him, and did not allow him to be swayed by the stereotypes of others. What a difference that made!

Ordained in 2002, Johnny Zayas has been with the CRC since 1991, and has found a balanced focus that feels right for him. He enjoys the denomination's strong scriptural position together with its non-legalistic expression of the faith. He is a self-taught, highly motivated individual who looks forward to what God will continue to do in the CRC, especially in the multiethnic and second-generation Hispanic community of the body of Christ.

WHAT ARE SOME CHALLENGES BEFORE US?

Diversity Within the Family

The tendency of folks not familiar with Hispanics is to lump them into one, big, happy family. Here's an important caution: *Hispanics are not all alike!* They do not all look alike, sound alike, think alike, behave alike, or even always like each other. There are significant political differences between them, just as there are between people in this country. There are language differences too: even though national language elements may sound similar, various cultures often use familiar words to convey very different meanings. There are differences between Hispanics indigenous to the Americas and Hispanics of European origin, differences that range from the hardly noticeable to the inescapable. In addition, of course, are the whole variety of factors that make for cultural differences in North America in general: educational levels, financial resources, political affiliations, generational differences, and even geography and weather.

Spanish, English, or Spanglish?

A pressing questions for Hispanic congregations everywhere is, "What language shall we use?" A growing group of Hispanics, represented by Johnny Zayas, faces the unique challenge of *Spanglish*. Simply defined, *Spanglish* is any form of Spanish that incorporates a lot of jargon and other words borrowed from English. Spanglish may pop up in conversation, music styles and lyrics, conversational or public speech, and even one's approach to worship. My difficulty with Spanglish is that when it is used, Spanish and English both seem to lose their punch.

The congregation I serve adopted the philosophy of "Spanish only," and I appreciate this focus and concern. We need to have a Spanish option before us constantly for two reasons. First, we need to reach out and facilitate the preaching of the gospel to those who are elderly and those just arriving on our shores. Second, we need to keep the Spanish option available for future migration

"We need to have a Spanish option before us constantly. . . ."

129

and for our young people who may prefer English today but want to return to Spanish tomorrow.

At the same time, I believe the English option has to be part of Hispanic ministry as well. I don't agree with requiring the church to be the teacher and guardian of a particular culture and language. That is the role and responsibility of families. The calling of Christ's church is to facilitate the good news about the hope we have in Christ alone. The longer Hispanics are in the United States, the more comfortable they will be with English. In fact, over time more of them will need English. And if our churches do not offer it as an option, at best we will lose many of our people to English-speaking churches—and at worst they will be lost to the Church entirely.

The answer therefore is not *either/or* but *both/and*. This issue cannot be forced, and acculturation tends to do its own thing—in time. My advice is for congregations to provide the options, and let the people choose the best course for their own spiritual life and growth.

A Worldwide Harvest Field

We have an incredible opportunity to reach a mission field God has brought to us and continues bringing to us. We can only expect that Hispanic immigration to the United States will continue for decades to come. And we can expect that each new wave will continue to maintain ties with their homelands: sending resources back "home," visiting home and families whenever possible, and continuing to welcome many who come to visit and even stay. Furthermore, we have much to learn about sharing the good news of Jesus with those neighbors—nominal Roman Catholics and others—who learned about God in their early years, but still need to meet the true God through personal, living faith in Jesus.

It is exciting to consider that the forty million-plus Hispanics in the United States today constitute an incredible human bridge of communication to the countries and continents south of us. If we continue to stay vitally connected to them, by

God's grace we will become a great army of Jesus' followers that will extend God's kingdom not only in the United States, but throughout all the Americas.

One of numerous CRC Hispanic congregations God is raising up in South Florida is *Piedras Vivas* (Living Stones). This group of believers had its roots in the Presbyterian Church in America and affiliated with the CRC in 1998. I, Pastor Manny Bersach, am their pastor.

Pastor Manny Bersach and his wife, Terri

God Will Provide

My wife, Terri, is a real estate broker for one of the largest real estate companies in the United States. Living in Miami, we have seen a market that has become very strong among the Hispanic population. This helps us to imagine the projection that over the next twenty years a full 50 percent of all homes sold in the United States will be sold to Hispanics! As the Hispanic population becomes more established, this also will present huge challenges to the Hispanic churches in terms of property acquisition and facilities development. Thankfully we have an almighty God who is fully in control, and who will provide with abundance as we trust him. When God instructed Abraham to sacrifice his son Isaac, Abraham obeyed—and met Jehovah Jireh, the God who provides: "On the mountain of the Lord it will be provided" (Gen. 22:14). I am confident that God will provide for our every need as we serve God and put him first (cf. Matt. 6:33).

The question is, how deeply will the CRC invest in this great mission? I am not asking if we will get into real estate. Rather, are we willing to share with our neighbors something that is *real* and that includes an eternal *estate?* Praise God that the CRC is on a great track, investing in and reaching out to this major people group that God continues to bring our way. May God provide leaders with the willingness and courage to follow wherever God leads!

Will we say yes, even if it requires sacrifice? Are we ready to think of others as better than ourselves, remembering Paul's instruction, "Be devoted to one another in brotherly love, give preference to one another in honor" (Rom. 12:10, NASV). Thank you agency colleagues, thank you classis leaders, and thank you CRC—for praying for us, and for coming together as a team assembled by God to reach out to Hispanics everywhere!

Note: Special thanks to Mrs. Viviana Cornejo for interviewing pastor Gilbert Varela and pastor Gerry Muller.

DISCUSSION STARTERS

1. What three countries have the largest Hispanic populations in the world?

2. What stereotypic adjectives are sometimes used by others to describe Hispanics? What adjectives would you use, based on your *personal* experience?

3. What do you know about Hispanic churches and ministries in your city and state?

4. How would you compare the acculturation experience of Hispanics today to the experience of immigrants from central and northern Europe fifty years ago?

5. What similar and differing patterns did you observe regarding the five Hispanic pastors introduced in this chapter?

6. What do you believe is the "ideal" language for ministry among Hispanics? Explain your answer.

7. In what ways might God be calling you/your church to advance the mission of God among Hispanics?

CHAPTER SEVEN

PARTNERSHIP IN GOD'S KINGDOM: KOREAN ETHNIC CHURCHES

Edward W. Yoon

"We have different gifts, according to the grace given us." —Romans 12:6

When God called Abraham and made a covenant of salvation and blessing with him, God promised that his blessing would flow through Abraham to all the nations (Gen. 12:3). In light of this divine promise for international blessing, we will trace how our God has been enlarging his kingdom sincerely and patiently through partnership between Korean ethnic Christian people and the Christian Reformed Church in North America since 1969.

WHERE DID WE COME FROM?

In 1876 Scottish missionary John McIntyre baptized four Koreans in Manchuria. From that seemingly minor response, the number of Protestant Christians in Korea has grown by leaps and bounds. The 200 Christians in 1890 had multiplied to 50,000 by 1905. An autonomous Korean presbytery was formed. By 1909 the church had swelled to more than 200,000 members. In 1940 there were 370,000 Protestants, and by 1995 the *Christian Year Book* of Korea reported nearly 14 million Protestant Christians.

Two major factors were responsible for waves of Korean immigration to the United States. The first was the political and economic hardship of Korea from the late nineteenth century through the early twentieth century, and the second was the establishment in 1882 of a treaty for amity and friendship between Korea and the U.S.

According to *The Christian Today,* a Los Angeles-based Korean newspaper, as of December 2004 there were 3,665 Korean-American churches in North America. Among them 41.6 percent are Presbyterian, 13.4 percent are Baptist, and 11 percent are Methodist. Geographically, 34 percent of the Korean-American churches are located in California; 10.7 percent in New York; 5.8 percent in Illinois; 5 percent in New Jersey; 4 percent in Maryland, and 4 percent in Texas. The Korean presence in Canada is comparatively small.

The development of the Korean church in the U.S. is related to three major waves of Korean immigration to the U.S. since 1903. The first wave was from 1903 to 1944; the second from 1945 to 1964; and the third began in 1965 and continues to the present. A law amended by the U.S. Congress in 1965 opened the door for any persons from any country to immigrate to the U.S. Most of the Korean churches in the U.S., including Korean ethnic churches belonging to the CRC, were founded during this third wave of Korean immigration.

HOW HAVE THE CRC KOREAN CHURCHES GROWN?
Some Korean Pioneers: 1969-1984

Rev. Myung-Jae Lee, pastor of First CRC

Rev. Myung-Jae Lee, who faithfully finished his ministry in 1992, listed three reasons for his long-time affiliation with the CRC:

• his theological position was consistent with the CRC

• he was grateful for ways in which the denomination gave him friendly guidance and support

• he appreciated his "autonomous authority" to lead the local church.

The Rev. Myung-Jae Lee planted a Korean church in Chicago in 1967 and joined the CRC in 1969. Various other Korean congregations followed his lead: First Toronto Presbyterian Church in 1977, Los Angeles Korean CRC in 1976, Orange Korean CRC in 1978, Phoenix Korean Presbyterian Church in 1981, Los Angeles Hanmi CRC in 1983, San Jose New Hope CRC also in 1983, and others.

In this early period (1969-1984), each Korean congregation joining the CRC was often the only

Korean-speaking congregation in the classis. Nor did the Koreans have a nation-wide organization to help them work together to address difficulties in dealing with the CRC arising from cultural and linguistic barriers.

Formation of the Korean Council: 1984-1993

After these early Korean churches joined the CRC in the 1970s, many more joined the denomination in 1980s. By 1989 a roster of Korean CRC member churches reported 40 pastors and 42 congregations. In response to a growing need for mutual fellowship and solidarity among Korean CRC churches, pastors and lay representatives from each of the congregations met together in July 1984 at Orange Korean CRC, Fullerton, California, to form the Korean Council of the CRC in North America. Rev. Yong-Chool Kim, pastor of First Toronto Presbyterian Church, was elected as the first moderator of the organization.

Since 1984 the Korean Council has convened annually. Although it is not an officially recognized structure in CRC polity, it has been used by God in building and sustaining a strong sense of community among CRC Korean leaders around the country. It also has helped integrate various opinions coming from the churches and leaders, and in several instances has been in dialogue with CRC denominational leadership. Most of the key leaders who served the Korean Council between 1984 and 1993 had been trained within either very conservative or moderate Presbyterian denominations in Korea, including allegiance to the Westminster Confession of Faith.

In order to more effectively coordinate the rapid expansion of Korean churches affiliated with the CRC, the Korean Council requested denominational assistance in establishing a Korean ministry coordinator position. Particularly with the assistance of Christian Reformed Home Missions, this position was first filled on a part-time basis by Rev. John T. Kim. After he decided to pursue doctoral studies at the Free University in the

Netherlands, he was succeeded by Rev. John Choi, who served from 1987 to 1997. By 1997 the position had become full time and was renamed Korean ministry director. The Rev. Tong Kun Park became the new Korean ministry director in 1998.

From the beginning, the member churches and leaders of the Korean Council were strongly interested in forming a Korean-speaking classis within the CRC. In 1987 the Korean Council first formally proposed to a classis and synod the formation of a Korean-speaking classis. An overture to this effect was consistently set forth, eventually culminating in synodical approval in 1996. This led quickly to the formation of a Korean-speaking classis, Classis Pacific Hanmi, which is located in the Greater Los Angeles area.

The CRC's struggle over the ordination of women to all church offices eventually became a controversial issue among the Korean CRC churches. At its 1990 annual meeting the Korean Council decided that each local consistory would determine its own position regarding the denominational position. However, not all members of the Korean Council agreed with this approach, and some spoke openly of their intention to leave.

By 1990 there were 35 Korean congregations scattered widely throughout the CRC.

Korean Congregations in the CRC (1990)	
Classis	Congregations
California South	14
Chicago South	1
Columbia	3
Central California	3
Florida	2
Grand Rapids North	1
Greater Los Angeles	11

For more effective coordination among the member churches, in 1991 the Korean Council annual meeting decided to form six local "chapters": Northern California, Southern California, North-Central U.S., North-West U.S., South-Central, and Florida. Regarding the ordination of women to church office, the Korean Council in 1991 agreed that the Korean CRC churches would delay any corporate decision until the CRC synod made a further decision in 1992. When synod approved the opening of all church offices to women, each congregation had to consider anew its affiliation with the CRC. Despite ardent persuasion by the denominational leadership team, in 1993 a number of Korean congregations decided to leave the CRC.

Going and Coming: 1993-Present

According to the 1994 Korean Council annual report, in the prior year at least six congregations—and 3,598 individual members—had left the denomination. This represented nearly 20 percent of the churches and half of the total CRC Korean membership. However, in the midst of such a traumatic church split, the Korean Council leadership demonstrated its unshakable loyalty to the denomination for the next decades.

Thanks to this unshakable solidarity and the sacrificial leadership of the two denominationally supported leaders, the Revs. John Choi and Tong Kun Park, the number of Korean CRC churches again began to increase. In 1998 the council reported sixty member churches. By 2002 it reported sixty-five congregations with a total membership of 5,637. And one year later the total had swelled to seventy-five churches with 7,111 members. As of 2005 the Korean Council tallied ninety-one congregations and 8,000 members.

Rev. Tong K. Park and his wife, Jane Jongsun

Rev. Tong K. Park, the third Korean ministry director and a CRC Home Missions regional leader, has provided servant leadership to Korean CRC churches since 1998. The expansion of churches from sixty to ninety within that time period is one mark of his excellent leadership. Special cause for praise is the fact that a dozen of these thirty new churches are led by 1.5- and second-generation Korean pastors. Rev. Park has persistently challenged the Korean CRC churches to enlarge their boundaries of ministry beyond their parochial limits in order to contribute to the overall ministry effectiveness of the CRC.

Most of these ninety-one churches are led by first-generation pastors; eight churches are led by 1.5 or second-generation pastors. Geographically, fifty-four churches are located in southern California (fourteen in Classis South California, thirteen in Classis Great Los Angeles, and twenty-seven in Classis Pacific Hanmi); ten churches in the northwestern region (eight in Classis Northwest, two in Classis Columbia); thirteen churches in the eastern region (eight in Classis Hackensak, three in Classis Hudson, and two in Classis Southeast); seven churches in the Midwest region and seven churches in other regions (including Canada).

WHAT KIND OF PEOPLE ARE WE?

People on the Margins

The Korean people, one of the northeastern Asian peoples, lived in the Korean peninsula for a long time. They are a monoethnic people with a common language called Hangul, similar skin color, and an established culture. Their unique ethnicity, with many of their Asian characteristics being very different from the historically dominant white culture in the United States, is a major reason that Korean people regard themselves as a marginal people in the American setting.

Of course, every ethnic group who comes to America may feel marginalized in their interactions with mainstream American society for a period of time, as the Dutch immigrants experienced before us. However, the experience of people from Korea and other Asian immigrants who came to America must be dealt with more seriously because of their unique ethnicity in terms of language, culture, and worldviews.

These difficulties led Korean CRC churches to pursue the formation of a Korean-speaking classis, beginning in 1985. The eventual formation of Classis Pacific Hanmi in 1996 reminds us that cultural and language factors for any ethnic groups must be taken into serious consideration by the denomination. In fact, in keeping with the CRC's strenuous efforts to enfold a variety of ethnic and racial groups, we need to further develop our theology in support of ethnic diversity and racial reconciliation.

People Accustomed to Suffering

Living between the superpower countries of China and Japan, Korea has been invaded numerous times by one country or the other throughout its history. As a result of these military invasions, countless Korean people were slain or captured and taken as slaves to either China or Japan. Throughout their history, political and military instability and geography made it impossible for Koreans to appropriately express the indescribable resentments and hurts resulting from the atrocities they suffered. Instead, these unexpressed grudges were internalized and given voice in roughly two opposite ways: through artistic expression such as developing various chants called "Pansori" and group dances called "Nong-Ak"; or through addictive behaviors such as heavy drinking, gambling ("Hwa-Too"), uncontrollable domestic violence, and so on.

In 1905 Korea became a protectorate of Japan. This national trauma caused many Koreans to turn to Christianity as the sole hope for their country and became one of the factors contributing to the great

"For the first immigrant Koreans who live in America, one of the greatest difficulties is a feeling of alienation and frustration caused by linguistic and cultural differences."

—Rev. Tong K. Park.

revival in 1907 and after. During the Japanese colonial rule over Korea for 36 years (1910-1945), many Korean Christians were arrested and tortured and even slain as a result of their protests against the Japanese enforcement of Shinto-worship.

People Rooted in the Confucian Worldview

Throughout history, the Korean people have been in contact primarily with four major worldviews prior to Christianity: Shamanism, Taoism, Buddhism, and Confucianism. The most dominant and controlling worldview for the Korean people was Confucianism, especially dominant during the Chosun dynasty from 1392 to 1910. Drawing from the Confucian worldview and ideology, the Chosun dynasty legitimatized dualistic social ranks. This is reflected in the dichotomy between nobility and the common people and the superiority of the male over the female. Also, the elderly deserved to be revered by the younger. Even the already-dead forefathers were to be venerated, according to the rigid Confucian social code. This Confucian worldview had a tremendous influence on Koreans' thinking and their way of life.

It is not difficult to draw a connection between the culturally engraved, authoritarian, male-superiority attitudes of Korean men over the centuries and the opposition of Christian Korean male leaders to the ordination of women to church offices traditionally filled by men only. While recognizing that the CRC has wrestled with this issue in light of biblical considerations, we also need to be aware of our inherited worldviews, and be willing to fully orient or reorient our thinking to the genuine spirit of the gospel as the Holy Spirit leads us.

People Engraved in a Presbyterian Ethos

Presbyterian missionaries to Korea heavily influenced the formation of the early Korean churches until the 1930s. Naturally the theology and polity of these western Presbyterian missionaries was based on the historic Reformed faith and

Korean Christians learned great endurance and perseverance through suffering. It is believed that the brutal rule of the Japanese resulted in fostering the spiritual disciplines of early morning prayers, Friday night prayer vigils, and fasting. Today most Korean CRC churches exercise such devotional disciplines; in fact, these may be one of their spiritual strong points.

Presbyterian polity. The fruit of their missionary work was seen especially in the staunch leadership of Dr. Hyung-Yong Park and his disciple Dr. Yune-Sun Park. These Korean guardians of the Reformed faith had a powerful influence on most of the CRC Korean leaders who came to America in 1960s and 1970s.

Upon coming to North America, many Presbyterian-trained Korean pastors sought affiliation with the CRC. Certainly they enjoyed affinity with the CRC in terms of the Reformed faith and theology. But there were other considerations as well. The Christian Reformed World Relief Committee had begun ministry in Korea right after the ravages of the Korean War (1950-1953). Calvin Theological Seminary developed strong relationships with a number of Korean seminaries in the 1960s. Another attractive consideration was that the CRC, itself an immigrant church, had been sympathetic to and very supportive of the ethnic immigrant churches.

What was not sufficiently understood was the depth of difference in church polity. The central structure-oriented polity of Korean Presbyterians often conflicts with the consistory-centered polity of the CRC, which in turn has become an internal ecclesiastical problem for the Korean CRC churches. In this regard, we as Korean leaders recognize that as members of the CRC, with its distinctive Reformed confessions and church polity, Korean churches have a responsibility to understand and embrace *both* the Reformed confessions *and* CRC church polity in order to be homogenous with the denomination in our faith and practice.

"The Seminary of the Korean Presbyterian General Assembly, now one of the largest seminaries in the world, still fondly remembers the support and encouragement of the CRC in the mid-1960s."

—REV. TONG K. PARK

What Are the Varieties of Ministry in the Korean CRC Community?

Worship in Transition

Most Korean congregations that are led by first-generation immigrant pastors use the Korean language during worship and in other aspects of their ministries. They usually follow a conventional order of worship, with only slight innovation handed down by western Protestant missionaries dating back to 1884. Exceptions occur increasingly within larger-sized congregations, who tend to offer greater variety in worship consisting of a blend of both conventional and contemporary worship. Usually the younger members prefer a contemporary mode of worship.

Most Korean congregations in America practice early morning prayer on a daily basis from Monday through Saturday and offer frequent night vigils. And most of them also hold an annual retreat for the congregation with a seasonal retreat for prayers.

When they decide to minister in the English language, Korean-American churches generally have used one of three alternate approaches. The first has been to initiate an English language ministry as one of the congregation's various ministry programs, still led and supervised exclusively by first-generation immigrant leaders. A second approach has been to develop a separate English-language ministry using the same church facility. A third option has been to start an independent English language ministry apart from the Korean-speaking parent congregation. We are not prepared to say which option may be the best, trusting that this will become clear to us over time in the light of God's blessing.

This third option, however, may well be the only option for achieving multiethnic and multiracial ministry. The Rev. G. Suh, one of a growing number of 1.5-generation (see sidebar on next page) Korean-Americans and a former missionary to Nigeria, serves as pastor of an English-speaking ministry of a Korean congregation in northern California. He observed that many Korean-American churches seem to function with an ethno-centric Korean mindset. He has seen this both in hesitancy to invite people from other ethnicities and racial backgrounds to their worship services, and in considering whether to appoint persons from another ethnicity or race to leadership positions in their local ministries. Rev. Suh also expressed the hope that the Korean-American churches will embrace a more concrete vision for multiethnic ministry and commit themselves to actualizing it.

Credentialing and Training of Korean Pastors

Most Korean pastors who came to the United States did so after finishing required theological training, usually a Master of Divinity degree, and pastoral experience in Korea. However, the one important dimension of training they could not bring with them was knowledge and experience of the diverse and complex postmodern, post-Christian cultures of their new homeland. Coming as they did from a rather homogeneous, monolingual and monocultural environment, most of these leaders have found themselves struggling with issues and problems common to immigrant churches. They have had to deal not only with differences in the acculturation of their immigrant parishioners, but also with all the other issues of life and culture that influence their homes, their communities, and the next generation. Trained under the traditional Korean Presbyterian polity and practices, they have often found it difficult to understand and apply the nuances of Reformed theology and practice that have developed over generations in the current cultural environment of the Korean churches.

One of the essential ways to address this difficulty is through training and education. However, overall CRC support in this area has been very marginal, if not seriously lacking, and the immigrant churches have often felt left "on their own" to figure out how to adjust to and comply with the traditional Christian Reformed ways of doing things. For example, for a long time Korean churches did not have access to the CRC Church Order and Rules for Synodical Procedure in the Korean language.

A 1.5-generation person was born in Korea but immigrated to North American at an early age, usually before the teen years. Korean persons born in North America as children of immigrant parents often refer to themselves as the 2.0 generation.

In the fall of 2005, a Korean translation of the *Manual of Christian Reformed Church Government* became available.

Without access to these materials in their native language, it has been very difficult to organize systematic training in a way that would be truly helpful to these leaders. First-generation Korean churches have continued to have a hard time understanding Christian Reformed polity and putting it into practice. However, their interest in CRC polity and practice has continued to grow, and some of these immigrant congregations have intentionally modified their current approaches to embrace CRC policies and practices. At the same time, if this transition is to serve the churches well, Korean leaders and denominational leaders as a whole need to communicate freely with one another in developing appropriate training procedures. It is important for all parties to listen to one another and respect each other. The goal after all is not that the Korean churches and various other ethnic and racial groups be "assimilated" into the dominant denominational culture, but rather that the various ethnic and racial communities within the CRC be mutually edified and enriched through their living and working together.

Coffee Break: Small Group Ministry in a Global Expansion (1990-Present)

Coffee Break, a small group evangelism ministry, was first introduced to the Korean-American churches in 1990. The occasion was a joint Korean-American workshop on basic leadership training held at Orange Korean CRC. Mrs. Myung S. Lee was the workshop coordinator for this memorable event, and through a divine encounter with international Coffee Break director Betty Veldman, Mrs. Lee became the first Korean Coffee Break ministry representative (serving from 1990-2001).

As the first Korean trainer for small group ministry in the Korean churches, she conducted about 150 basic leadership training workshops throughout the United States, as well as in Brazil, Canada, China, and Korea. Mrs. Lee was also instrumental in planting several regional Coffee Break centers through southern California in Anaheim, Buena Park, and South Bay. From 1990 through 2001,

God blessed these efforts by introducing small group evangelistic ministry in many Korean-American churches. In response to the growing need for empowering small group leaders, in 1997 Mrs. Lee initiated nationwide Korean Coffee Break Conferences, which have continued bi-annually since then.

Mrs. Myung S. Lee, the first Korean Coffee Break ministry representative

In 2001 the leadership mantle for Coffee Break ministry was passed on to Mr. and Mrs. Kyu and Grace Paek. Under their leadership, one interesting development has been the formation of Coffee Break small groups for men. Leadership training needs also have continued to mushroom on many fronts. In 2004 Mr. and Mrs. Paek, with Dr. Edward Yoon as Coffee Break consultant, sponsored a leadership training conference for Coffee Break workshop speakers. God blessed this training by raising up five new Coffee Break workshop leaders who are energetically serving this movement in China and Korea as well as the U.S.

As of 2005 the Korean Coffee Break small group ministry in North America is served by a ministry developer team, one consultant, twelve international workshop speakers, twenty regional inter-denominational centers, and hundreds of small groups at local churches.

Voice of the Reformed: a Korean **Banner?**

In 1992 the Korean Council, with the support of the fifty-five Korean member churches, decided to publish *Voice of the Reformed*. This bimonthly Korean language magazine was designed to foster communication among the Korean churches and between the churches and the CRC. When controversial issues such as the formation of a Korean-speaking classis and the proposed ordination of women to church office were being debated among the churches, *Voice of the Reformed* played a mediating role for the Korean churches and helped them move toward consensus.

Rev. Bomsu Kim, editor of *Voice of the Reformed*, with his wife, Aesook

In a personal interview Kim made these two bold suggestions for the future of the denomination:

• CRC leadership needs to appoint more minority ethnic leaders, beyond the present Caucasian-concentrated leadership, for denominational-level ministries.

•CRC leadership needs to reevaluate the relationship between the denomination and *Voice of the Reformed*, which has an uncertain status in the denominational structure.

Rev. Bomsu Kim became the editor of *Voice of the Reformed* in 2002. Under his leadership the magazine was redesigned and its circulation expanded to 2,500. Sponsored by the Korean Council, with twenty-seven primary supporting churches among eighty-seven member churches, *Voice of the Reformed* celebrated its hundredth edition in August 2005.

By way of such ministries as Korean Coffee Break and *Voice of the Reformed*, the Korean CRC community has been enlarging its range of responsibility and influence. CRC Korean leaders are thankful to the denomination for its encouragement and boldness in releasing much authority and autonomy to multiethnic and multiracial churches within the denomination.

Conclusion

In light of God's universal covenant for all the nations, we dare to believe that the Korean people have been coming to America since 1903 as part of God's providential guidance. It was this divine guidance that led Korean people to plant many churches as spiritual and emotional havens for their people. It was this divine guidance that designed the Christian Reformed denomination to be a universal covenantal community of God with the desire to embrace other ethnic and racial

groups. And it was this divine providence that prompted some of God's Korean covenantal community to relate with the CRC since 1969.

Over these thirty-plus years there have been misunderstandings, conflicts, mistakes, and even "separations" in our interactions. Yet we are convinced that God led Korean people into the CRC not just to participate but to partner with the denomination, in order to be used as God's humble vessels for the greater growth and expansion of his kingdom.

Thanking God for everything he has given us as the Korean community in the CRC, we eagerly accept new challenges and assignments as members of our denominational covenantal circle. We are committed to understanding more accurately the "DNA" of the CRC, its ethos and polity, and are determined to contextualize these in ways that fit with our Korean ethnicity and culture. We accept our unique identity within the CRC covenantal circle as passionate missionary instruments of

Pastor Jin So Yoo of All Nations Church

Pastor Jin So Yoo is senior pastor of All Nations Church in Lake View Terrace, California. Begun in 1996, All Nations affiliated with the CRC in 2003. As of spring 2005, All Nations was hosting four Sunday morning services in their new facility. Pastor Yoo described the first service as more devotional, the second and third similar to one another, and the fourth as "very loud." About 2,000 adults and 1,000 youth and children have been gathering weekly for worship and instruction, giving All Nations the largest attendance of any CRC congregation. Passionate about mission, All Nations operates its own Bible Institute in Mexico and supports nine fulltime missionaries—five in Mexico and one each in Argentina, Canada (among First Nations people), China, and the Ukraine.

God's universal covenant. We pray for the greater incoming of all the nations, and desire to be better equipped to more fully embrace and share ministry with all other ethnic groups as God brings us into relationship with each other.

As we faithfully go about doing what our God has assigned to all of us, someday we will see God's promises fulfilled as described in Revelation 7:9-12. This "great multitude that no one could count, from every nation, tribe, people and language" will gather before the throne of God and the Lamb and praise God forever and ever!

DISCUSSION STARTERS

1. Korean churches started to join the CRC denomination in 1969. In what ways was the CRC denomination ready or not ready to enlarge its circle to other ethnic and racial groups?

2. In what ways has the formation of the Korean Council in 1984 served the interests of Korean Christian Reformed member churches? Should a CRC organization like this continue indefinitely? Why or why not?

3. The Korean Christian Reformed member churches have experienced some conflicts and church splits during these thirty-plus years. What do you think the Korean community or the CRC as a whole has learned about addressing and resolving church conflicts?

4. The Korean CRC community, like other ethnic groups, has the unique challenge of embracing CRC theology and principle-based practice while at the same time celebrating its own ethnic identity and cultural flavor. What kinds of strategies and approaches can help the various ethnic and racial groups within the CRC to meet this unique challenge?

5. What biblical and theological considerations give us reason to believe that at some point in history all the nations who have been chosen and called by God will be gathered together to praise our triune God forever?

CHAPTER EIGHT

SCATTERED AND GATHERED: ASIAN-AMERICAN STORIES

Lois and Mike Vander Pol

"I was a stranger and you invited me in. . . ." —Matthew 25:35

In 1885 France gifted the United States with the now famous Statue of Liberty. For more than a century Lady Liberty's lamp has brightened the New York harbor with the invitation "Give me your tired, your poor, your huddled masses yearning to breathe free. . . . Send these, the homeless, tempest-bound to me. . . ." Ironically, the welcome of these words was withheld from various people groups for generations. Nevertheless, this invitation to the world warms the hearts of old and new citizens alike. Especially after World War II, and again after other international military actions, Christian Reformed congregations in the United States and Canada have welcomed and sought to enfold immigrant and refugee folks from around the world.

This chapter tells the stories of new immigrants and refugees of Asian origin (other than Koreans, whose story is told in chapter 7) who are seeking a church home in the CRC. Their languages, cultures, and customs may be quite different from those of the CRC's dominant culture, but together we are children of one Father, and sisters and brothers in God's diverse and uniting family. How have persons from Asian countries been welcomed into Canada and the United States? What kind of experiences have they had in Christian Reformed congregations? How are we the multiracial and multicultural body of Christ together?

WHAT BROUGHT ASIAN IMMIGRANTS TO THE UNITED STATES?

Immigrants usually come to their new country under less stressful circumstances than refugees. Generally they know who their sponsors are and where they will be settling. Often they know who will welcome them at the airport. Today some immigrants even come for a preview trip and thus have some idea about what to expect when they arrive.

The first immigrants in the Christian Reformed Church, the ones who founded it, were primarily of Dutch origin, with some folks of German roots sprinkled in here and there. Over the generations, additional ethnic groups to join the Christian Reformed Church included people from mainland China and from other parts of Asia.

Chu Hsuen (Paul) Szto at ordination, 1957

Rev. Peter Sing Sui Yang

The story of Rev. and Mrs. Peter Yang among Mandarin-speaking Chinese in San Francisco is a wonderful story of God's leading.

Rev. Yang was brought up in China by Christian parents who "served the Lord faithfully with great distinction." In Peter's first year as a junior high student, he confirmed his faith that Jesus was his personal Savior: "I began

Many Chinese immigrated to the U.S. and Canada following World War II, with the first opening of citizenship to Chinese people. One of those immigrants was Chu Hsuen Szto, known to us as Rev. Paul Szto. Pastor Szto, the first Chinese minister in the CRC, was ordained into the ministry in 1952 and has served the Christian Reformed community for over fifty years. Another veteran pastor in the CRC is Rev. Peter Yang, who in 1963 launched Golden Gate CRC in San Francisco. Both of these men are influential leaders and godly examples in the CRC. Both had contact with Christian missionaries in China and embraced the Christian faith before immigrating to the U.S.

As a result of their contact with Christian missionaries, immigrants from the Philippines joined the CRC family as well. In the Philippines the predominant religion has been Roman Catholic since the time of its colonization by Spain. Pastor Albert Sideco, who pastors the Filipino CRC in New Jersey said, "I grew up a Roman Catholic. I knew Jesus but was a nominal Christian. I didn't know the Bible and was not enthusiastic about Jesus. I worked in Saudi Arabia as an engineer, and there missionaries led me to Jesus. The text that moved me was Acts 16:31, 'Believe in the Lord Jesus Christ and you will be saved, you and your household.'" Pastor Fernando del Rosario from Hayward, California, attributes his coming into the CRC to his relationship with Rev. Maas Vander Bilt, a CRC missionary in the Philippines from 1979-1989.

"WHY ARE THEY SO KIND TO MY PEOPLE?"

"Who are these people who are helping us? And what motivates them to give and give and give?" So spoke Pastor Socheth Na, evangelist of Cambodian Fellowship in Holland, Michigan. He was in a refugee camp and noticed how people who were unable to speak his language were handing out blankets and food, helping with passports, and taking people to the pharmacy to buy medicine. His story is similar to that of many others, a story of God calling through the faithful love expressed in the lives of Christians.

When he was in high school in Cambodia, Socheth heard about the Christian faith. Across from his school was a Christian church, and every day he saw young people reading the Bible under the shade of a coconut tree. At that time, what raced through his mind was, "Traitors! They are traitors to our Buddhist homeland as they call Jesus Lord, rather than recognizing our king as king." However, these Christians did not have much impact on him, for he was more interested in obtaining his degree than in learning about a new religion.

my volitional search of God's will for my life." After graduating from Calvin Seminary, he was appointed by Christian Reformed Home Missions as a missionary among the Chinese. He was examined and approved for ordination by Classis Los Angeles in 1963.

Sensing the need for ministry in San Francisco among "the largest Chinese settlement in North America," Pastor Yang asked the Classical Home Missions Committee to support a new ministry there. Although the initial response was negative, Pastor Yang's own extensive research was convincing. In 1964, with the support of Home Missions and the classis, the Yangs began a new ministry among the Chinese in San Francisco. The dedicated steering committee from Walnut Creek CRC, Pastor Yang's calling church, gradually replaced themselves with Chinese elders of the new church.

Today Golden Gate CRC has a weekly attendance of around 450 people and is a vibrant Christian witness in its multiethnic neighborhood with a community outreach program for all ages every day of the week. Golden Gate staff and volunteers come from Christian and non-Christian backgrounds and have a passion for welcoming and enfolding members of their community.

"I am grateful to our heavenly Father for his guidance and his provision to minister in the Christian Reformed Church," Pastor Yang declared. "Much can be said for the many who helped me out of their sheer kindness. Praise the Lord."

Pastors Socheth Na and
Albert Sideco

Then, in November 1979, he came to the refugee camp and saw Christians again. They provided food; cared for those wounded by bombs, land mines, and grenades; they comforted the sick and distributed blankets. Who are these people, and why do they do these good things for us? he wondered.

During his stay in the refugee camp, Socheth worked closely with a foreign doctor named Barbara who prayed with him, treated him kindly, and shared the gospel daily, but he did not commit his life to the Lord. He was more interested in getting to the United States or Australia to study. Nonetheless, he says, "She created doubt in me about Christians. Who are they? Why are they so kind to my people?"

He explains, "Because I wanted to go abroad, I went to a Christian church to learn some Bible, because most of us who lived in the refugee camps learned that when you become a Christian they will take you to the U.S. or to Australia." By his own testimony, he felt the Lord touching his life but did not then answer the call. He was a "carefree person" during this period of his life. He gives one illustration that shows his attitude. His brother had become a Buddhist monk, and his sister told him to bring some food to their brother. Usually, when bringing food to the monks, you would bow three times. Socheth went to the temple. "My brother was waiting for me and I gave the food to him—without bowing." Another monk demanded, "What did you do? You didn't bow."

Socheth replied, "No! Even though he is a monk, he is my brother." In a deep sense, he alienated himself from his relatives. "I was not very religious. All I cared for was my school and my books. Perhaps once a year I would go to the temple, more for fun than to worship. I was a carefree person."

The story of Pastor Na can be repeated by many of the other refugees who came to the U.S. during and after the Vietnamese war and the later battles in a number of Southeast Asian countries—Laos, Cambodia, and Vietnam. Many of the refugees who came to such places as Holland, Michigan; Minneapolis, Minnesota; and the various points of entry in California were born and raised Buddhist. Others were born into Christian families. Refugees often navigated extremely complex spiritual, political, economic, and cultural passages when coming to America.

How Does a Vietnamese American Pastor Build a Church?

Pastor Nam Kieu and his wife, Lien, escaped from Vietnam in a small boat with her family. Their journey was long and filled with danger, deceit, and drama. Eventually they arrived at a refugee camp in the Philippines, and from there they were able to come to the U.S. in 1979.

Pastor Kieu's father was a Christian pastor in Vietnam with the Christian and Missionary Alliance Church, which no doubt influenced Pastor Kieu's own desire to study for the ministry. In the greater Los Angeles area he was encouraged for a time by the Rev. Bao Nguyen, and enrolled at the International Theological Seminary in Los Angeles. Upon his graduation, and with the encouragement of Dr. John Kromminga, who was then serving in his "retirement" as president of ITS, Pastor Kieu studied at Calvin Seminary.

In 1991 Pastor Kieu and his wife, Lien, settled in San Jose and began their Christian Reformed ministry with the initial sponsorship of Christian Reformed Home Missions. The new church, named Liberty CRC in the spirit of freedom from the tyrannies of sin and suffering, gathered mostly nonbelievers coming from Buddhist backgrounds. At first the ministry was heavily focused on helping refugees resettle. In the process, people were invited to worship, to study the Bible, and to receive baptism. Many adults, teens, and children offered their lives to Jesus Christ and worshiped God. This story is an exception among the refugees from South Asia, for most refugees that came to the CRC were Buddhists.

Knowing that the Vietnamese people are very concerned about their children's education, Pastor Kieu organized a successful after-school program and a morning preschool program. Both programs, averaging 300 students per day, met in a rented commercial building that was used for church worship on Sundays. Every day the children sang praises to the Lord and were introduced to Bible stories. Liberty has sponsored many events to reach out to the Vietnamese community with the gospel and to gather the family of God among the Vietnamese in San Jose.

In late summer 2004, just before school resumed, Liberty suddenly lost its lease on its building. Pastor Kieu and Lien experienced a loss of their twelve-year effort to build a vibrant church and school ministry with a huge impact on the community. For a time Pastor and Mrs. Kieu ceased from active ministry to reflect and seek healing. Kieu is now focusing on a fresh vision of how his Liberty experience can help him plant multiple churches among the Asian Americans on the West Coast.

CAN ONE PERSON MAKE A DIFFERENCE?

The lives of many families were cruelly disrupted by the war in Vietnam and the war in Cambodia, causing many to flee. Parents were sent to the farm while their children were placed in child care. Death was always close at hand. Many people have stories to tell about how they were saved from death a number of times. One such story is told by Pastor John Kim of Khmer CRC in Denver. He had been sent to work on a farm and was responsible for plowing a field with the help of a cow. The cow got away. The punishment for letting the cow get away was death, but one person with some authority had compassion on John and interceded to save his life, saying that the cow might come back. The cow did come back and John's life was spared. Sometimes even in the refugee camps people feared for their lives. Many died, but many others survived to lead their people and the CRC in the new land.

Most of the refugees received by the CRC settled in Central and Southern California, Michigan, Minnesota, and Colorado. One such refugee, John Kim, and his family were among fifty families sponsored by Third CRC in Denver. Pastor Kim attributes his coming to the Lord and to leadership within the CRC to an elder and his wife, who were members of Third CRC. This couple felt that John was called to the pastoral ministry, but he wasn't convinced. They prayed together. Initially he had no idea of becoming a pastor. He worked at a fast-food restaurant, and later as a machine operator. But because Kim felt compassion for his

Berkhof and Calvin in Vietnam

After some years in the United States, Pastor Kieu returned home to Vietnam to visit his parents. With him he took two books about the Reformed faith he had embraced to give his father. Because his father was a Christian and Missionary Alliance pastor, Pastor Kieu was a bit fearful of what his father would say about his being Reformed. As they settled down over a cup of tea, Pastor Kieu hesitantly pulled out the two books, Berkhof's *Systematic Theology* and Calvin's *Institutes*. His father examined the books, put them down, and walked out of the room to his study. A little later he came back with two well-marked books, *Systematic Theology* by Louis Berkhof and *Institutes of the Christian Religion* by John Calvin. Relating this story still brings tears to Pastor Kieu's eyes.

Young people at Khmer CRC

people in the Denver area, he quit his job and took some courses with Gary Teja of Christian Reformed Home Missions. After that experience he made himself available for pastoral ministry.

This same elder also challenged and encouraged Pastor Socheth Na to enter ministry by asking him to translate as the elder preached to the Cambodians. He also provided him with study materials, and suggested that he visit Reformed Bible College in Grand Rapids, where he later prepared for ministry as an evangelist.

These and other stories teach us that the Lord often uses relationships and the backing of a gracious and supportive church family to make a huge difference in the destiny of many others.

Another story: Phonh Sinbondit landed in Chicago with his family and only five dollars in his pocket. They eventually ended up in Ohio, where Sinbondit found a very good managerial position in a factory, but he felt the Lord calling him to work among the Laotian people in Holland, Michigan. With the encouragement of Home Missions, on weekends he traveled to Holland to preach and teach. In 2004, Pastor Sinbondit was called to the Lao ministry in Minneapolis. He retired from his job and entered fulltime pastoral ministry among the 20,000 Laotian families in the Minneapolis/St. Paul area, where some of the big problems are drugs, alcohol, and very low high school graduation rates.

These issues are addressed in the youth group in Pastor Sinbondit's church. Another problem in the area is low-paying jobs. People have to work long hours to support themselves, which limits the time they have for family life and education. The community is in trouble. In this environment the church presents a different lifestyle and a different attitude. The church is in contact with many people, offering friendship and care in times of need. With family counseling and interpreter services as ongoing ministries to the community, the church is growing. The church knows that it is possible for God to bring light where it's hard to see, and to make a way when there is no way. Classis Lake Superior provides prayer and financial support for this ministry.

WHAT ARE SOME UNIQUE CULTURAL CHALLENGES?

The Challenge for Asian Americans

Whether one is American born of Asian descent or an immigrant or refugee from Asia, functioning in relation to the dominant culture can be challenging and complex. Historically, Asian persons arrive with a culture very different from that of their new home.

Differences Between Asian and North American Cultures	
Asian Culture	**North American Culture**
Elders are highly respected and obeyed.	Elders are often addressed by their first name.
Family is extended family in multi-generational households.	Families are separated into "nuclear" households.
Government and religion are often intertwined.	Government and religion are separate.
The poor have little or no authority in decision-making to influence society.	Decisions are often made through a democratic process.
The priest or religious leader oversees religious life of the community.	People are encouraged to decide individually about their own spiritual well-being.
Social community is within walking distance or an easy bus ride.	Social community often is highly dependent on automobile transportation.

First-generation leaders often have been treated badly by the dominant culture and customs of their new North American neighbors. When Pastor John Kim moved into his home in Denver, one of the neighbors threw eggs and rocks through his window. The church context also can be disappointing. At some classis meetings, Asian-American pastors sit in the back row and are not involved in the discussions. Lack of a shared language and lack of patience or cultural flexibility on the part of the dominant group often contributes to this lack of participation.

Pastor Socheth Na speaks highly of the gifts and generosity of Graafschap CRC, a congregation that has helped him and his people in many ways. However, the road wasn't always smooth. He tells the story that when he first wanted to reach out to the Cambodians living in the Holland area, he proposed to have lunch in church after the worship service because "that's how we attract people," but it was about four years before he was able to implement his plan because the leadership at Graafschap CRC adhered to a long-held cultural conviction that "we don't have lunch in church after the worship service on Sunday."

The Vietnamese are a small group in the CRC, with a total of 150-200 members in the four churches. Each church struggles to survive and has little opportunity to associate much with the broader CRC. Because the older people do not speak or understand English, the young people are isolated from them and their wisdom. Our prayer is that young people will retain their Asian American culture even as they also become conversant in the dominant American culture.

Sharing a common language appears to be essential to beginning to understand one another in the face of cultural misunderstandings and misconceptions. Adapting to the dominant American culture widely varies. On one hand, a pastor says, "I'm learning as much as possible to become American"; on the other, a first-generation immigrant is afraid and never ventures out of the house alone. One congregation member says, "Sorry to say that as a church body, we have not been immersed in any significant way with the CRCNA"; another says, "I'm learning all about the Dutch Reformed faith so that I can relate."

The Challenge for Asian-American Pastoral Leaders

Christian Reformed Home Missions hosted the Asian Planning Group from 1999 to 2004 to enable Asian pastor representatives from the various Asian groups to discuss common issues and communicate the results of their meetings to the other pastors of their ethnic group. The members of this planning group came from various religious backgrounds and received theological training in various ways: at Reformed Bible College, Calvin Theological Seminary, or by individualized training with the pastor of their parent church. Members of the planning group generally were quite isolated from other immigrant or refugee groups from their own home country because of the geographic spread of their sponsoring families or sponsoring churches. Because of their geographic isolation, these

planning meetings also served as a source of personal encouragement for these brothers and sisters in the Lord.

With the assistance of a Sustaining Pastoral Excellence grant funded by a Lilly Foundation grant to the CRC, the Asian Planning Group has evolved into an Asian American Pastoral Ministry

Asian Pastoral Ministry Group, left to right: Esteban Lugo (Race Relations director), Matthew Le, San Sok, Socheth Na, Gil Suh, John Kim, Albert Sideco, Tina Sideco, Mike and Lois Vander Pol (advisors), Vickie and Fernando del Rosario, Nam Kieu peer learning group. With a second year of funding approved, the group is committed to providing ongoing leadership training and encouragement for Asian-American leaders within their networks.

Notwithstanding their varied levels of training and differing ministry contexts, participants have many similar concerns, including health care coverage, adequate pension, and the need for improved church facilities. In most cases, the spouse of the pastor works outside the home to help provide for the family. In some instances the pastor has other work to supplement insufficient compensation. Another common concern is the decrease in worship attendance among younger members. It's possible that they are not connecting culturally with the first generation, or that the church is not connecting culturally with them.

As part of their mutual encouragement, the meeting enables pastors to nurture one another through studying the Word together and to sharpen each other through sharing their ministry skills. Each meeting also includes time for pastors to sift through traditional Asian ways and those of the dominant American culture in order to help their congregations to follow Jesus. Another ever-present concern is to identify and develop new leaders who can bridge the generation gap. Group members are conscientious about their opportunities and responsibilities toward the denomination they have chosen to join. As Asian-American leaders, their prayerful goal is to be active partners in denominational life at congregational, classical and synodical levels.

THE CHALLENGE FOR PERSONS FROM THE DOMINANT CULTURE

What can we do better? We can be more patient, more flexible. We can respect and appreciate the image of God in persons different from ourselves. When the person speaking to us is struggling with the English language, we can sit back and listen.

Instead of putting the whole burden for communicating on the newcomer, we can accept responsibility for listening in order to understand. In the words of the apostle Paul, we are to "accept one another, then, just as Christ accepted you, in order to bring praise to God" (Rom. 15:7).

When persons from the dominant culture have the opportunity to listen to persons from another culture, this Chinese character reminds them to open their ears, close their mouths, receive with their hearts, and regard the speaker as a child of the King. After all, Christ died to bring people together (Eph. 2:13-15). So, particularly for those who are members of the dominant culture, encountering someone from another culture is an opportunity to humble ourselves before the other person, trusting the Holy Spirit to enrich our life through this person God has placed before us.

> When you talk you only repeat what you already know, but if you listen you may learn something.
>
> —AMISH PROVERB

As part of this listening, God calls us as Jesus' followers to become involved in the lives of persons who may be seeking spiritually. Immigrants and refugees often are very curious about Christianity and want to learn more about the God of the Bible. It is important for those of us who already know Jesus to learn as much as we can about the lives and culture of those who may be spiritually seeking. Developing relationships in this way will open doors for introducing people to

The Chinese character for "listen" is a combination of four parts:
• an ear that is open,
• a mouth that is closed,
• a heart that is receptive,
• the character for royalty.

"Answering before listening is both stupid and rude."
—PROVERBS 18:13, THE MESSAGE

Jesus in culturally meaningful ways, while also enriching our own understanding of life in Jesus. This is what Paul was talking about when he said, "I have become all things to all men so that by all possible means I might save some" (1 Cor. 9:22). As a servant of Jesus Christ, Paul identified with people in their own cultural context in order to help them come to see and know Jesus through their own cultural lens. The more culturally experienced we become in our understanding of Jesus, the more mature we will become in our relationship to Jesus—as individual Christians and as a multiracial church.

DISCUSSION STARTERS

1. What do we learn about the Christian witness from the story of Pastor Socheth Na while he was in his homeland and in the refugee camp?

2. Discuss how you experience multiethnicity in your workplace and in your neighborhood. Can principles for one setting be used effectively in another area?

3. What biblical principles will challenge persons from the dominant culture of your congregation to be more inclusive of persons from other cultures in areas of church leadership and governance?

4. Do you believe God is calling your congregation to become more multiracial and multicultural? If not, why not? If so, what practical actions can your church take?

5. Romans 15:7 tells us that we give praise to God by accepting one another. Discuss how and why that is true.

CHAPTER NINE

EMBRACING PEOPLE OF COLOR IN CANADA

John VanTil

"Dear children, let us not love with words or tongue, but with actions and in truth." —I John 3:18

In 2005 the Christian Reformed Church celebrated the one-hundred-year anniversary of the founding of the first Christian Reformed congregation in Canada. Prior to World War II, the number of CRC congregations in Canada remained very small. After the war, however, the CRC in Canada grew rapidly. As a result of major emigration from The Netherlands in the late 1940s, 1950s, and 1960s, it mushroomed toward its present size of around 260 congregations. This post-World War II wave of immigrants built church facilities, started Christian schools, and formed Christian organizations. Once these efforts had been reasonably established, they began looking around them with the question, How shall the CRC in Canada fulfill God's calling to "go and make disciples of all nations" (Matt. 28:19, NIV)? We can find answers to this question by listening to the stories of outreach ministry to communities in Canada that consist primarily of persons of color.

CAN FIRST NATIONS CULTURE BE REDEEMED?

I arrived in Canada in April 1953, and for the first two years worked on a farm just outside Brampton, Ontario, now part of the greater Toronto area. The record of

Early Outreach Ministry by CRC Canada

• The Canadian CRC has been motivated by compassion for the "hurting" more than by concern for the "lost."

• Second-generation Dutch Canadians focused their early mission efforts on people of other races and cultures.

• Early CRC outreach initiatives were toward persons in greater need than themselves: First Nations people in the cities and refugees from Cambodia, Laos, Vietnam, and, more recently, the Sudan.

The term "Indian" is a historic misnomer for Natives in North America, dating back to Columbus, who first thought he had discovered India. The indigenous people in Canada are commonly—and respectfully— referred to as aboriginal or First Nations people. The First Nations people often have been clustered with the Metis, a large biracial Canadian population of persons from aboriginal and French origin (Metis is a French word for "mixed"). The Metis frequently were affected by the dominant culture in ways similar to First Nations people. In this story the terms are used interchangeably.

my baptism was sent by the *Gereformeerde Kerk* in the Netherlands to Immanuel CRC in Brampton. A couple of years later I stood before the Immanuel congregation and made profession of my faith in Jesus Christ as Savior and Lord of my life.

During the summer months, when the pace of farm work allowed it, I would go to "downtown" Brampton to see what was going on. As in other towns and cities in Canada, it was not unusual to see intoxicated people lying in gutters along the streets, many of them "Indians" (as we called them then). These folks caught the eye of newly arrived Dutch Canadians such as myself. Part of our Dutch Reformed inheritance was a strong sense of compassion for the needy and empathy for the underdog. We were aware that among many Canadians the aboriginal people were often viewed as savages—uneducable and unwilling to work. As newly arrived immigrants we did not share that history or that viewpoint.

Over the years the Canadian government had tried to deal with the "Indian problem." With the cooperation of mainline churches in Canada, First Nations children were removed from their homes and placed in boarding schools. Based on the view that they were savages, the boarding schools were designed to "civilize" them. Separated from their parents and home communities, these children were forbidden to speak their own languages and were required to learn the dominant culture of white people. Christian teaching also was forced upon them as part of the civilizing process. This went on well into the 1960s. In recent decades stories have surfaced regarding the horrific sexual, physical, emotional, and spiritual abuse and suffering of these children.

Indian Family Centre—Winnipeg

In the mid-1960s CRC churches began talking about possible ministry among Canada's first residents. By 1968 the Council of Christian Reformed Churches in Canada was asked to investigate starting a ministry among Indians and Metis. In 1970 the council established a quota of

$1.00 per family "for mission work among the Indians." In 1972 it appointed a committee to hire a Christian worker "preferably of Indian extraction" to begin this outreach ministry. The mind of the council delegates was expressed in the sentiment that "action is what the Lord wants, not more study." They also mentioned the great commission in Matthew 28 as Christ's marching orders for CRC Canada. The three Christian Reformed congregations in Winnipeg, Manitoba, were eager to host a Canadian Urban Hospitality House, and the council accepted this proposal.

Henk De Bruyn at his ordination in 1965

After an unsuccessful search for a person "of Indian extraction," the council appointed Pastor Henk De Bruyn as the first director. De Bruyn was an immigrant from the Netherlands and a graduate from Calvin College and Calvin Theological Seminary. His prior ministry experience included a missionary pastorate in Fredericton, New Brunswick, and an interim assignment among African Americans in Detroit, Michigan.

The Winnipeg Indian Family Centre opened in 1974. From the beginning, De Bruyn was urged to form a worshiping community. De Bruyn's recollection is that the ministry was to be "spiritually and socially oriented." For a while he gathered a small group of Native people for Sunday worship, and his wife, Fran, taught Sunday school for the children. De Bruyn noticed, however, that as soon as the worship time concluded at the centre, the Native "congregation" would then walk over to the nearby Stella Mares United Church for a group meeting of their own. To De Bruyn, the worship gatherings were not effective and did not last much beyond that first year, according to the following interview:

VanTil: We are exploring the relationship between congregations with a predominantly white membership and congregations with persons of color. So why did you not seek to establish a congregation among the aboriginal people in Winnipeg?

De Bruyn: When I reflected back on my ministry experience with African Americans in Detroit, I remembered the CRC white folks that were involved in that ministry. They were very dedicated and strongly committed to working with African American people. But when it came to making decisions, it was the white people who decided what was to be done. I also noticed that when a choir of African Americans performed in the church the place was rocking, but when we sang from the *Psalter Hymnal* it was all very subdued. I decided that I needed to help the aboriginal people find a safe place where they could celebrate their own culture and where they could make their own decisions. So I always kept the (white) CRC people at arm's length. We tried to make culturally sensitive decisions, helping the aboriginal people redeem their own culture and allowing it to be cleansed by the Spirit of God.

VanTil: How do you compare this approach to CRC ministry initiatives among people of color in the United States?

De Bruyn: When the CRC did missionary work with the Navajo people and later among African Americans, the question always forced on the people was, "How do we fit into the CRC?" In my view, when there is dependency on funds, there always is manipulation. This is what I was determined to avoid in the Indian Family Centre. Although funds were coming in from the CRC, we fostered an attitude of gratitude but also allowed us (sic) to be ourselves.

VanTil: What in your view is the greatest contribution that the Indian Family Centre made?

De Bruyn: We developed a focus of ministry that sees culture as a gift from God that is redeemable. Therefore we do not join an organization that already has its own culture-specific focus.

VanTil: Where does Jesus Christ fit in with this?

De Bruyn: The Spirit of God reveals Jesus Christ in ways that people can appropriate. We are simply the conduit through whom that happens. Most Native people in Canada are aware of Jesus Christ; they were raised in mission schools. But they do not know the power and healing of his grace. I cannot make that grace happen in people, the Spirit does that. But I believe it happens, for example, in our worship circle. We read a Scripture and then people reflect on it from what they see and experience. Gradually people begin to experience wholeness and grace.

VanTil: Do they come to faith in Jesus?

De Bruyn: It is not important that people name the name of Jesus Christ. Often the people will refer to "the Creator," for example. The bottom line for me, ever since I entered this ministry, is that there is only one healer in personal and community life and that is Jesus. The dark side does not heal. When I see healing, that is Christ at work. If I can name this healing as the healing of Christ, that makes me a dynamic Christian. But a dynamic Christ does not need to be advertised.

Aboriginal Ministry—CRC Canada

Subsequent to birthing the Winnipeg ministry, CRC Canada started two more ministries to aboriginal people: the Indian Metis Christian Fellowship in Regina, Saskatchewan, and the Edmonton Native Healing Centre in Edmonton, Alberta. The Regina and Edmonton ministries, with Bert Adema and Chaplain Harold Roscher as directors, respectively, are more clearly Christian ministries. Although they are not church planting ministries, they foster strong relationships with the CRC and its members. These ministries seek to bring healing into the lives of broken people, and there is evidence that this is happening.

Staff at Indian Metis Christian Fellowship, left to right: William Davison; Bert Adema, director; and Carol Kirk, counselor

Helping Canadian aboriginal people redeem their culture is a unique feature of all three ministry centres. All offer midweek worship that involves gathering in a circle. During worship Scriptures are read, people are encouraged to reflect on the Scriptures, and prayers are invited and offered. Most circle gatherings start with the smudge. An aboriginal elder lights a mixture of sweet grass, sage, tobacco, and other ingredients. He then moves from person to person in the circle holding the smoldering mixture before each of them. The participants use their cupped hands to cover themselves with the smoke while praying that as the smoke covers them, so may the Spirit of the Creator cleanse every part of them. Often the leader explains that the Spirit is the Spirit of the Creator who is Jesus Christ. The ministries also have taken steps to redeem the sweat lodge. While participants are seated in the closed sweat lodge, they are encouraged to reflect on the grace of God in their lives—or other subjects that will help them humble themselves before the Creator and seek his forgiveness and blessing.

In 1968 CRC congregations in Canada were asked to pray for an aboriginal person to lead a ministry to Canada's aboriginal people on behalf of the CRC. That very year a baby boy was born of an aboriginal mother; he was eventually adopted and reared by a CRC family as Harold Roscher. On January 1, 2005, Roscher became director of the Edmonton Native Healing Centre. God works in mysterious ways. Roscher values his Reformed upbringing and believes that his task in life is to reconcile Christian and aboriginal teaching and culture.

Smudge sticks

WOULD YOU BLESS A CHINESE CHURCH PLANT?

"OK, John, this is what we do when we lay the groundwork for starting a new congregation for Chinese people," they said. "We invite the pastors of Chinese congregations to a lunch. Over a nice

Paul Lomavatu
Caribou Community Church in Williams Lake, British Columbia—a church plant—is the only CRC with a sizeable number of aboriginal Christians. Pastor Paul Lomavatu reports that one-third of the members are aboriginal Canadians.

lunch we introduce the CRC, explain our intention for starting a new church among the Chinese people, and then ask for their blessing on our project." This was the advice of CRC pastors Peter Yang from San Francisco and Stephen Jung from Los Angeles. I was the CRC Home Missions regional leader for Canada, and Classis British Columbia had authorized us to explore the potential for a new church among the Chinese in the greater Vancouver area.

Pastors Yang and Jung also gave me this lesson in pastoral etiquette. "After we finish eating and the pastors have given their blessing to our effort, we'll close the meeting with prayer. Now, we Chinese like to argue over who pays the bill. Just let us have our friendly arguing for a while, and then you pay." So right after the prayer the pastors began reaching for their wallets and saying, "I'll pay," "I'll pay," "No, let me pay." After a little while I said, "Brothers, today you are the guests of Christian Reformed Home Missions." As I pulled out my credit card, their wallets disappeared quickly.

With the assured support of CRC Home Missions and classis British Columbia, pastor Stephen Jung was called to start a Chinese-speaking church in Richmond, British Columbia. In 1979 Pastor Jung and his wife, Sue, moved from the U.S. to Canada to begin the work. Sue Jung remembers lots of hard work, entertaining many people in their home, and visiting many others in theirs. The Jungs expanded their circle of influence and kept on inviting people into fellowship with the Lord Jesus and the newly forming church. The Lord honored their work and many prayers, and Immanuel CRC was born.

The people first reached were primarily those who spoke Taiwanese (a Chinese language also known as Fukienese or Amoy). As the congregation continued to grow, it developed an excellent facility. Today the congregation has three worshiping groups, one each in English, Mandarin, and Taiwanese. Immanuel became an organized CRC in 1984. Pastors have come and gone, some of them not speaking English very well. But Immanuel Church leaders attend classis meetings faithfully and participate in its activities.

First CRC of Richmond had offered the use of their church facilities for the Chinese language members. Members of "First Church" had sponsored a number of Vietnamese refugees, and in the early days of Immanuel CRC, Pastor Jung also reached out to them. In a few years' time this ministry grew into an Asian Canadian congregation located in Abbotsford, British Columbia. Adopting the name Zion, this group of believers

also became an organized congregation of the CRCNA.

During the 1980s and 1990s three efforts were made at church planting among the Chinese population in Toronto, Ontario. Two of these were very short-lived. The third, Toronto Chinese CRC, led by Pastor Timothy Chan, existed for fifteen years. It came out of the Toronto Lighthouse Ministry, an inner-city diaconal ministry sponsored by the classis. However, unable to become a viable congregation, it was discontinued in 2005.

Whether church plants flourish or wither away involves multiple factors. In the case of these plants, certainly "the harvest is plentiful"—God provided sincere Christian pastors supported by wonderful Christian spouses, and all three ministries were supported generously by Classis Toronto. Other factors may be less clear: was the CRC prepared to help appropriately, were the pastors a good fit for their specific communities, were these efforts in God's own time, and the like. Leaders of future church planting initiatives will do well to consider the experience of these and other church planters.

How Shall We Love the People of the Nations?
All Nations Christian Fellowship
"It was the lowest part of my life," Marcia Martin recalls. It must have shown on her face, because as

Verney Kho and her family
Verney Kho was born in the Philippines. Her parents, although not Christians, sent her to a Christian school for a good education, and she became a Christian. In the 1970s, Verney and her husband, Ben, immigrated to Canada. In 1983 she started helping a friend teach Sunday school at Immanuel CRC in Richmond, British Columbia. She kept on learning more about the CRC, and eventually became a deacon. Soon after that, she was asked to substitute for an elder as a delegate to classis. When the classis voted not to seat a woman delegate, prompting some delegates to walk out, other delegates apologized to her. Her personal view was, "Being from Asian paternalistic family background, I respected their decision." Since then, Mrs. Kho has been seated on the board of Christian Reformed Home Missions as well as of the CRCNA Board of Trustees. And at the CRC synods of 2004 and 2005 she served as an ethnic advisor.

she was riding the Toronto subway in 1994 a stranger said to her, "You're in lots of trouble; may I pray with you?" The person offering prayer was Lena Santiago, a member of All Nations Christian Fellowship. Lena asked if Marcia knew Jesus, and Marcia said she did. But then Lena asked, "Have you accepted him as your personal Savior?" When Marcia admitted she had not, Lena led her to do so. "Bam," says Marcia, "I joined the team and it changed my life." Four years earlier Marcia had come to Canada from the Philippines and worked as a nanny. Shortly after meeting Lena, Marcia became a member of All Nations Christian Fellowship.

How did All Nations come into existence? In the summer of 1968, CRC folks conducted a vacation Bible school in the Palmerston area of Toronto. The VBS was well received and was repeated the next year, leading to Bible clubs for boys and girls. By 1971 a drop-in centre for teens had been started, and Pastor Ken Verhulst came on to the scene as leader for what was later named "The Lighthouse." As the ministry expanded into other areas of need, many CRC members volunteered. By the late 1970s, CRC congregations also began sponsoring refugees from Southeast Asia, and soon The Lighthouse began providing English as a Second Language classes, a food bank, and used clothing.

The Lighthouse ministry grew in numbers and in diversity. An expanding number of persons from Southeast Asia began meeting for worship on Sunday mornings. A group of Cantonese-speaking folks from China began meeting on Sunday afternoons. Initially Ms. Rita Wong was hired to serve the morning group, and Timothy Chan, a theological student from Hong Kong, was hired to serve the Cantonese-speaking folks. Eventually Patrick Paas was called and ordained as pastor for the people primarily from Southeast Asia—which then become All Nations Christian Fellowship—and Timothy Chan was ordained to lead the Toronto Chinese CRC. Both groups experienced initial growth and had to find other venues for hosting their meetings.

All Nations Christian Fellowship moved to rental facilities in Glen Rhodes United Church. There they meet on Sunday afternoons for worship and to hold Sunday school for children and youth. The worshiping community, a wonderfully diverse group of people from many nations, numbers around fifty on average. All Nations continues to have guests who are not yet followers of Jesus, but everyone always experiences fellowship and love. In 1997 Pastor Paas left for health reasons; since then the church has been served by part-time pastors. The first was Pastor Tim Berends, who served the congregation while he was on staff with InterVarsity Christian Fellowship in the Toronto area. The second was Pastor Ray Samaroo, who came to Canada from Guyana. Samaroo joined the CRC under Berends' prior ministry in Winnipeg, and was ordained there as an evangelist. When Samaroo moved to Toronto a few years later, Pastor Tim Berends introduced him to All Nations. At this writing Samaroo still serves as part-time pastor of All Nations.

All Nations became an officially recognized congregation in the CRC during 2004, an achievement members are excited about. Marcia Tran is one of the deacons. Worshipers at All Nations get a taste of what it must have been like in Jerusalem on that first Pentecost Sunday. One difference, however, is that in Toronto the people at All Nations are from Brazil, China, Guyana, India, Japan, Korea, The Netherlands, the Philippines, and Vietnam. Another difference is that they all hear the Word of God and sing praises to their Savior Jesus Christ in their second language. But like those Christians on Pentecost, there is much joy among them!

Ministry among Cambodian Refugees

Of the many thousands of refugees who came to Canada during the 1980s and 1990s, a sizeable number came from Cambodia—often after spending several years in refugee camps in Laos. In St. Thomas, Ontario, just south of London, numerous Cambodian refugee families were sponsored by folks from First CRC. Two important

CRC congregations in Canada sponsored several thousand refugees and their families. A number of them were "processed" through The Lighthouse.

Among the refugees was a young Vietnamese man named Phu Tran. While in a refugee camp in Hong Kong, Phu Tran became a follower of Jesus Christ. He was sponsored by Rehoboth CRC and became a regular presence at The Lighthouse. There he met Marcia, and eventually the two married. When he began attending school in Toronto, he supported himself with part-time custodial work at First CRC in Toronto. Sometimes Marcia would help Phu with his work. One day as she was cleaning the sanctuary, a group of people came in. It struck her that they were all white people, and that no one said anything to her. "They only looked at me; I felt weird about that," she recalled. No one made comments that "put her down," but she did not feel warmly welcomed.

Another couple, Ed and Cathy, also were brought together by The Lighthouse and All Nations. Ed Boekee was a long-term volunteer at The Lighthouse and a long-time CRC member of Dutch origin. Cathy, like Marcia Tran, came to Canada from the Philippines.

servant-leaders were Robert Holtrop, a deacon at First, and Rudy Boys. The emphasis was on helping people escape the refugee camps for a new future in Canada. Once refugees arrived and were being settled, they were asked about other family members. When potential new refugees were identified and vouched for by family members already in Canada, the congregation would endorse their sponsorship. Hundreds of refugees came to London and St. Thomas through this process.

Few, if any, of these refugees were Christians in Cambodia. Many of them heard about Jesus Christ and the kingdom of God while in the camps in Laos, and many of them embraced the faith. Upon their arrival in Canada the CRC provided worship services designed especially for them.

In London local CRC pastors and other ministers conducted these services, at times with as many as fifty or more people attending. The Home Missions Committee of Classis Chatham encouraged classis to support these efforts, and eventually Good News CRC in London took ownership of the work.

In St. Thomas there was a more concerted effort to train Cambodian pastoral leadership. Like so many others, San Sok had fled from Cambodia with his family and spent three years in a refugee camp in Laos. During their stay in the camp, San Sok and his wife were taught about Jesus Christ and became believers. Sponsored by First CRC of St. Thomas, Mr. Sok showed great interest in growing as a Christian and being part of the church. Eventually the church ordained him as an elder and assigned him the task of caring for members of the Cambodian community. That still is his assignment. Meanwhile, he and his wife also continue their employment as factory workers.

Recently Elder Sok was invited to join the Asian American Pastoral Ministry group. This group meets once or twice annually for spiritual growth and skill development as leaders among their people. Elder Sok is very encouraged by this opportunity.

Were all these efforts too little and too late? Would more refugees have responded differently if local pastors had been more involved? Should the classis have invested more deeply in training indigenous leaders? Gradually the members of the Cambodian Canadian committee have reverted to their pre-refugee culture and faith. At First CRC in St. Thomas, where a separate worship service is offered for the Cambodian community, Mr. Sok and his entire group can fit in the council room. And at Good News CRC in London, the attendance of former Cambodian refugees has all but ceased.

Friendship Community—Diverse from Day One

Fred Witteveen

Fred Witteveen was born in Canada and was baptized, catechized, and made profession of faith at Willowdale CRC near Toronto. With one year left in his studies at Calvin Theological Seminary, Witteveen contacted Christian Reformed Home Missions about doing some preliminary work for a possible church plant in Toronto, Ontario. In the summer of 1990, Witteveen was granted a summer assignment in the Toronto area for conducting an assessment of opportunities and needs in "high need" communities. With three such communities identified, the choice was made for the Jane-Finch area—in large part because of its proximity to three established CRC congregations in the Toronto area: Rehoboth Fellowship, Second Brampton, and Witteveen's home church, Willowdale.

Friendship Community was started in 1991. Reportedly the Jane-Finch area had the highest crime rate. Income levels were far below the national average. A high percentage of Jane-Finch

Only two families in Friendship Community can point to a Reformed background: the Witteveens and the Pullenayegems. The Chris Pullenayegem family is from a Reformed Church in Sri Lanka. Before they came to Canada, Chris searched the Internet for a Reformed church in Toronto. Friendship Community showed up on the screen, and it became their church home.

When asked why people come to Friendship Community, Chris explained, "They come because they are invited by family or friends, and they stay because they get a warm welcome, the environment is friendly, and there is a wonderful diversity of people of color."

How does Friendship Community "fit" within the CRC family of churches? Witteveen acknowledged that this is a real challenge. "To be enfolded you need cultural linkages to the host church," he said. "That's why we are actually targeting some people from the CRC, so that we can integrate better. The host culture is not coming our way, so the enfolding process is very difficult, integration is very difficult." Pullenayegem observed, "There are two sides to that coin; Friendship is a model of how churches can be intentionally diverse. We don't have the leadership resources to grow to large numbers. I don't see us becoming a church of 200-300 people." He adds, "The CRC counts church health by numbers. We may well become a church with many satellite churches all through Toronto."

Friendship Community is not yet an "organized" CRC congregation, and therefore is not eligible to have voting delegates at the meetings of Classis Toronto. Usually Witteveen attends those meetings alone as the "missionary pastor." Pullenayegem would like to see the classis invite and seat delegates from emerging churches such as Friendship Community, even if those churches are not yet organized.

Friendship Community is *the* most culturally, ethnically, and racially diverse CRC in Canada. Like All Nations, it reminds us of the international assembly the apostle Peter preached to that first Pentecost Sunday, except that in Toronto everyone hears the Word in English. May this great work of the Spirit of God through Friendship Community inspire and challenge all congregations located in multicultural settings to faithfully witness among the diverse peoples of their surrounding communities.

residents were new to Canada, and the community was culturally and racially diverse. So from day 1, like the church of Antioch in Acts 11, Friendship Community reached out to people from different languages and nations. On a typical Sunday morning, the sixty to seventy worshipers include persons from Argentina, the Bahamas, Burundi, Cambodia, the Caribbean, China, Colombia, Eastern Europe, Ecuador, Grenada, Guyana, India, Jamaica, Kenya, Korea, St. Vincent, Sri Lanka, and Uganda. Surely the Spirit of the Lord is in this place!

DISCUSSION STARTERS

1. Is it important for people to specifically name the name of Jesus?

2. Harold Roscher wants to "reconcile Christian and aboriginal teaching and culture." Is that kind of reconciling the calling of every Christian from every culture? Why or why not?

3. What factors may have contributed to the demise of the three attempted CRC church plants among Chinese people in Toronto?

4. Marcia Tran noticed that no one said anything to her when she was cleaning the sanctuary. What would you have said?

5. What lessons would you draw from CRC outreach ministry to Cambodian refugees in the London and St. Thomas communities?

6. What opportunities do you see for your congregation to pursue and experience more racial and cultural diversity?

CHAPTER TEN

LEARNING TO COUNT TO ONE:
SIGNPOSTS TOWARD BECOMING A
MULTIRACIAL CHURCH

Alfred E. Mulder

"Our many-ness becomes our one-ness—Christ doesn't become fragmented in us. Rather, we become unified in him." —1 Corinthians 10:17, The Message

The Christian Church in North America is incredibly divided. Organizationally the CRC is separate from hundreds of other Bible-believing denominations. And, like most denominations, the CRC is mostly divided along racial lines. Of its nearly 1,000 congregations in 2005, about 800 are exclusively or predominantly white, and another 150 exclusively or predominantly persons of color. Only about forty CRC congregations—that's four out of one hundred—are multiracial.

Before going to the cross Jesus prayed for his followers: "Holy Father, protect them by the power of your name . . . so that they may be one as we are one" (John 17:11). Paul may have been thinking of Jesus' words when he wrote about the meaning of the one loaf in the Lord's Supper: "Our many-ness becomes one-ness—Christ doesn't become fragmented in us. Rather, we become unified in him" (1 Cor. 10:17, *The Message*). Church families have long known how to add and subtract, divide and multiply. Lord Jesus, teach us to count to one!

WHAT DO MULTIRACIAL CONGREGATIONS LOOK LIKE?

The all-too-common reality is for a majority racial group to impose its culture on persons among them from other cultural backgrounds. Some researchers suggest that a congregation begins a significant transition toward becoming multicultural when no one racial group accounts for more than 80 percent of the membership. This is the yardstick we have chosen to identify multiracial congregations in the CRC. In this chapter we focus on five such congregations.

> A congregation begins a significant transition toward becoming multicultural when no one racial group accounts for more than 80 percent of the membership.
> —DeYoung, Emerson, Yancey, and Kim, *United by Faith*, Oxford University Press, 2003, p. 3

Bethany CRC, Gallup, New Mexico

Missionaries were first assigned to Gallup in the 1930s. Bethany Church was the first group of Navajo believers to organize as a Christian Reformed congregation with all Navajo elders and deacons. That was in 1956 (also see chapter 4). When I became their pastor in 1968, Bethany had about seventy-five members, seventy of them Navajo. But that would soon change!

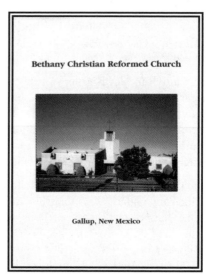

Bethany Christian Reformed Church

Gallup, New Mexico

Bethany CRC, Gallup, New Mexico, building dedicated in 1971

The consistory had asked for leadership, among other things, in reaching out to the Gallup community—note this—*including white folks!* So when we left Gallup in 1984, Bethany still numbered about seventy Navajo members—some "old" faces, some new. But these seventy Navajo members were encircled by a sea of two hundred white persons. Prompted by the Spirit and the civil rights movement, this formerly all-Navajo congregation had become multiracial, with its founding members in the minority.

With the stress of this rapid transition now history, and under the consistent teaching of long-term pastor Keith Bulthuis, Bethany's racial composition is increasingly diverse—with Navajo participation also increasing.

Pullman CRC, Chicago, Illinois

Started by the Chicago Tract Society in 1921 as an outreach to Lithuanian immigrants, this ministry was taken over by the four Roseland CRCs in 1926. Moving from changing neighborhood to changing neighborhood, in 1955 the ministry located at 105th and Corliss and became the Pullman Gospel Center.

Black folks first began worshiping at Pullman in 1968. This was around the same time that white Roseland residents began their mass exodus to the suburbs, accompanied by a corresponding influx of black families. Many of these families were looking for a new church home, contributing to Pullman's further racial transition.

Pullman received its first ordained pastor in 1972. It relocated to East 103rd Street in 1976, organized as a Christian Reformed congregation in 1980, and celebrated a new sanctuary on Easter Sunday 1987. The congregation has 250 members with an approximate black/white ratio of 60:40. Pullman's music director, Helen Breems, is a classically trained white sister who learned gospel music for the sake of the gospel. Rev. Rick Williams, of Panamanian origin, has been Pullman's pastor since 1981, serving as solo pastor since 1986.

Madison Square Church, Grand Rapids, Michigan

Madison traces its roots to 1914, when Pastor Van Wyk of Oakdale Park CRC began work among poor Appalachian whites in Madison "hollow." Although the cross-cultural opportunities changed with the changing neighborhood, Madison's ministry has always retained a focus on the poor and disenfranchised. Appropriately, its early leadership included lay leaders, women, and a pastor who was blind.

In the 1960s the small, mostly black congregation was joined by socially conscious white people. It organized as a Christian Reformed congregation in 1970, and was served by its first African American pastor, Rev. Virgil Patterson, from 1974 to 1977. From 1981 through 2004, Madison was led by black and white copastor teams: Rev. Dante Venegas and Rev. David Sieplinga, Venegas with Rev. David Beelen, and Beelen with Rev. Samuel Reeves.

Madison's membership swelled to 1,000 in the 1990s. In 2005 its worship attendance ranged from 1,100 to 1,400, with its racial composition estimated at 70 percent white, 25 percent black, and an emerging mosaic of persons of African, Asian, and Hispanic origin. In 2005, when Samuel Reeves decided to return to Liberia, David Beelen became solo pastor and team leader, complemented by a multiracial preaching team, a multiracial ministry staff, and a racially balanced council.

First CRC, Vancouver, British Columbia

First CRC of Vancouver was the first Christian Reformed congregation in British Columbia. Organized in 1926, First Church helped birth other CRCs, including its first daughter church in Houston, B.C., in 1939. By 2005 there were forty-four congregations in the province, many of them with a diminished but still discernible Dutch accent.

In the 1960s, on the heels of World War II, First Church swelled to nearly 1,000 members, cramping its valuable but modest-sized facility. Many of its white members followed the real estate market to outlying areas. More recent immigrants, many of them persons of color, moved into the neighborhoods surrounding the church.

Rev. Henry Numan

As membership dwindled, the leaders at First Church decided to share their space and their lives with persons racially and culturally different from themselves. In 2005 First Church still was 75 percent white. But under the grace-filled shepherding of Pastor Henry Numan (1976-1986 and 1999-present) its 200 members include persons of Chilean, Chinese, Czech Republic, Ethiopian, Fijian, Indonesian, Iranian, Italian, Filipino, Pakistani, Polish, South African, and Vietnamese origins.

In a recent three-year period First Church celebrated twelve adult baptisms.

Spirit and Truth Fellowship, Philadelphia, Pennsylvania

In June 1987 Rev. Manuel and Blanca Ortiz and Rev. Randy and Sue Baker pulled up stakes from Chicago, where they had planted churches and schools, only to drive them deeply into urban Philadelphia, where God was calling them to a new work.

Starting with home Bible studies in January 1988, Spirit and Truth Fellowship incorporated as a multiethnic, youth-oriented, inner-city ministry in 1989, and spun off the Ayuda Community Center in 1992. In 1996 Spirit and Truth located in East Hunting Park and began Hunting Park Christian Academy. The congregation "organized"

Mural at Hunting Park Christian Academy, partner ministry of Spirit and Truth, Philadelphia

as a Christian Reformed congregation in 1999. By 2002 it had sent out three elders and twenty-eight members to start a new church in nearby Germantown. And by 2005 Spirit and Truth Fellowship reported 135 members, with 300 persons attending Sunday morning services.

The rich diversity of the congregation, with no obvious numerical cultural or racial majority, also is reflected in its youthful staff—some of whom are African American, Hispanic, Portuguese, and Korean. Some also are preparing for future church planting service under primary pastor and mentor, Rev. Ortiz.

WHAT'S DOES IT TAKE TO BE A MULTIRACIAL CONGREGATION?

Note: It was an immense personal blessing to interview the pastor and several members from each of the five multiracial congregations described above. All spoke with caring and candor out of their love for the Lord and the church. With the exception of the pastors and a few others, the quotations in this section are given anonymously.

A Mission Heart

Gallup: "Bethany functions well because people want to reach across cultural lines." A teacher from Spirit and Truth: "God was preparing me from a young age to be a multicultural leader." Pastor Williams: "The Lord gifted me, starting way back in childhood, for this type of ministry. . . . In my inner being this is who I am. It really fits." First Vancouver: "We are moving more and more to an inclusive direction." But this is more than desire, and more than gifting. According to Dr. Manny Ortiz, "It's a giftedness in matters of mission; a calling to be enthusiastic about God's gift to the world." The heart of God is a mission heart.

Rick Williams

"The Lord gifted me starting way back in childhood for this type of ministry."

Openness to Persons from Other Cultures

"Be humble, be a learner!" "It requires a lot of sensitivity and gentleness." "We all need to do a lot more listening." Bethany folks cautioned, "There's not that common background knowledge, so we have to make fewer assumptions." Again, "It's more an attitude of openness than anything; it's always important to be aware of the diversity in the congregation." From Spirit and Truth: "At one point, when I was trying to teach this racially diverse group of kids to love themselves as the persons God had made them to be, God brought me to realize I needed to accept the same truth for myself, as flawed as I was. . . . We need to humble ourselves. And when we do, when we become the learner, the results are amazing."

Multiracial Intentionality

Folks mentioned this especially in relation to worship and leadership. Helen Breems of Pullman: "The fact that we are multiracial motivates and dictates everything that we do." Pastor Bulthuis: "We need to be extremely careful of our language. We never want to suggest that there is an 'inside' group. . . . Every part needs to be inclusive." Pastor Beelen: "We need to be intentional about breaking the leadership circle open over and over again. Acts 6 is our model for this." Laura Carpenter, on staff at Madison, observes: "Our staff and council are multicultural because we are committed to it. In our care groups, however, there is minimal intentionality about it, and there is minimal participation by persons of color."

Cultural Flexibility

On preaching: "If we were suburban white, more logical, less emotional, I would follow my notes more. But because we are multiracial, I try to communicate more visually." Another: "I've had to learn to be more of a narrative style preacher." Still another: "I've learned to preach without a manuscript, which enables me to be more responsive to the context." A musician on leadership: "It teaches you to be sensitive to a lot of different cultures, to be open, to want to learn." A pastor: "It forces you to become a student of other cultures, to develop a flexible personality. . . . I've had to learn to be flexible, and to enjoy being flexible."

WHAT'S ESPECIALLY CHALLENGING ABOUT MULTIRACIAL MINISTRY?

From a large variety of challenges—and not a little pain!—here are three that stand out.

Stretching Our Comfort Zones

Helen Breems confessed, "I was a snooty, classically trained musician. . . . When I was interviewed by the choir and considered the challenge of leading in African American music, the only thing I could tell them is, 'What I can give you is a heart that

"You cannot have a multiethnic church if you do not have multiethnic leadership. Otherwise you're always going to have some people who feel like they are visiting someone else's church."
—SUE BAKER, SPIRIT AND TRUTH

loves the Lord and a spirit that's willing to learn.' So I denied everything I knew and let them teach me. . . ." Gallup: "Indian Christians lost something by becoming a multiracial church. . . . Sometimes the Native people are not comfortable. They have all these problems they think white people don't have. So we Navajos sit in the back corner, feeling left out. But that's better now. . . ." Madison: "We want to have multicultural worship. To accomplish that we need to ask ourselves, 'Are you ready to give something up?' It's not easy. We all need to expect to be uncomfortable part of the time."

Achieving Authentic Shared Leadership

All five churches voiced the challenge of recognizing, recruiting, and supporting persons of color in leadership roles, and the importance of accomplishing authentic leadership development.

For persons of color it can be an internal and external struggle. A Navajo person: "I know my stuff in the workplace, but am afraid I'll say the wrong thing at church." An African American: "The challenge of persons of color is that we feel we need to meet the white standard, and suspect that we have sub-knowledge and are sub-prepared compared to white folks' standard." A Hispanic leader observed that most anywhere in the CRC, a person of color who aspires to become a credentialed leader in the CRC would do well to recruit a white leader as guide. One of Madison's copastor teams realized their proposals to council received more favorable action when presented by the white partner.

A white elder: "We don't always have to be in control. We need to be intentional about stepping back, listening more, being more patient, and encouraging others in expressing their insights and gifts." Pastor Bulthuis observed that this struggle has been going on ever since Acts 10, with Peter and Cornelius: "What is essential to the heart of the gospel and what isn't? It is so important to be in constant dialogue with God's Word about this, trying to discern what's important and what's not—without all our cultural baggage."

God, the Father of all people
you have called us to be one;
grant us grace to walk together
in the joy of Christ, your Son.

Challenged by your Word and
  Spirit,
blessed with gifts from heaven
  above,
as one body we will serve you
and bear witness to your love.

—CF. PSALTER HYMNAL 322. FIRST WRITTEN BY AL MULDER IN THE EARLY 1970s AS A POETIC VERSION OF THE MISSION STATEMENT OF BETHANY CRC, GALLUP, NM

Victoria Gibbs, Council Co-chair at Madison Square

"The issue of race sits at the table with every move. My perception is that I am seen as a black woman first, and as a leader second. Which means I'm being second-guessed by everybody, like I have to prove myself, like even black folks are asking: 'Who died and put you in charge? Who made you qualified?' A person is more likely to be struggling with these issues in a racially mixed setting."

Trust Across Racial Divides

An African American man who "married white" told of getting questions like these from white church members: "Why do (your) people do things that way? Why all this gospel music? Why do we have Black History Month every year?" Pastor Williams saw it from the other direction too. "People have their difficulties anyway, but when you add a layer of race and class, there's that much more. 'The white folks changed it up,' and 'They're just that way.' What saddens me is this deep suspicion of African Americans toward whites." Having grown up in Panama, and not having experienced racism as deeply, he admits to being surprised sometimes at the deep distrust of African Americans toward whites. "Even the best of them still cannot trust them." A white elder said, "Trust is a large issue. It simply takes longer to develop relationships in a multicultural setting." A black elder agreed: "Lots of times we're not patient enough with our brothers and sisters. Jesus Christ has a lot of patience with us, so I pray that each and every one of us would have that patience."

—Laura Carpenter, Director of Diversity and Worship at Madison Square and a credentialed antiracism trainer

ARE ALL THE CHALLENGES WORTH IT?

In a nutshell, most people who hang around multiracial congregations speak of being greatly blessed socially and spiritually, usually both. Here's one sample from each!

> Church used to be so structured, not even being allowed to turn around. Now the church has all kinds of people in it, people from all denominational backgrounds. I just feel proud of the diversity they bring. The band is playing. When they're all singing and there is this harmony, it is so wonderful, it feels so good.
>
> —BETHANY

> My priority is my kids, and this is hugely important for them—for moving forward in the working world, in their schooling, understanding other cultures, being comfortable with racial diversity. Some would argue for all white and all black, but we live in one world.
>
> —PULLMAN

David La Vizzo, his wife, Ruth, and Ryan, Amber, Zachary and Deanna

We're a very happy family . . . on Sundays and through the week. We're so enriched by all these people from such a variety of backgrounds. We are excited about witnessing and participating in all these adult baptisms in the past couple of years.

—Vancouver

When the pastor gave this personal illustration of white privilege, this was a highlight for me as a black person because it said to me: "We're going to speak the truth in this body of believers. We're not going to keep on dealing with the same old issues in the same old way . . . and expect different results. We're not playing games here; we're serious."

—Madison

It gives me a much fuller understanding of who God is, of what worship is. . . . All this diversity is from God. I enjoy more fully who God is; it's just such a huge blessing.

—Spirit and Truth

ARE MULTIRACIAL CONGREGATIONS MORE BIBLICAL?

Yes, I really did ask that question.

Obviously there are situations in which being multiracial may not be possible. There are rural areas with little or no racial diversity for miles around. Another example may be first-generation folks with language needs. Dr. Ortiz, whose day job is serving as a seminary professor, told of a student from New York City who identified fifty different ethnic groups in his city, all of which had at least one newspaper in their native language. No doubt worship services in New York are being conducted in as many different languages.

Granting those exceptions, but having tasted the multiracial experience, some simply know this is right for them. "Who am I to judge? All I know is that worshiping in a multicultural setting shows me more of who God is. He's God to African

Many first-generation folks will affiliate only with a ministry that speaks their own language.

Americans, to Hispanics, to whoever is here. It tells me about the expansiveness of the God whom I serve." "Not having this would be missing out on this unbelievable variety in God's creation. This is a little bit of what heaven will be."

Others argued that if physically possible it's also the right thing to do! An African American: "We tend to think that only *some churches* are called to do this. But in fact, all churches are called to do this *as God gives opportunity*." An Asian American: "You cannot be in Gallup and not serve the whole spectrum and think that you are being faithful. Besides, if every one was just like you, you might begin thinking that God must be just like you. It is so enriching to see that God is so much more diverse and rich himself." A white person: "I do not assume that all the persons of color have chosen to come here because they love it. In some ways they would be more comfortable not doing it, but they're doing so out of a sense of what God is calling them to do." Another white member: "Seeing all these white people moving further out into the suburbs just breaks my heart. One of the housing developments is actually called 'The Enclave.' What about our calling as Christians to love one another? How can Christians not even want to live next to Christians of another color?"

Pastor Beelen believes that multiracial congregations are a unique demonstration of God's transforming power. "A multiethnic church is proof that the gospel works. In a way the church is the only place now where being multiethnic is

"I think God really takes joy in a multicultural church, in seeing barriers broken down."
—JOSE FIGUEIREDO, SPIRIT AND TRUTH

David Beelen
"I love the phrase 'we must be accurate previews of coming attractions.' We are to become attractions of the completed kingdom of God."
—PASTOR DAVID BEELEN

discretionary. So when people actually *choose* to be together in this way, it speaks clearly to the power of the gospel." More than that, according to Beelen, this is God's plan for his kingdom. "In Revelation God makes clear what we are headed for. Christ is magnified and glorified in the gospel all the more when he appeals to people from every nation and background. Christ's glory shines with greater brightness and clarity in a multiracial setting."

Dr. Ortiz contends that in any and every context, ultimately it's about fulfilling the mission of God. "The Lord's agenda is one of inclusiveness and bringing the nations to himself," said Ortiz. "That is not optional. So even if the soil is homogeneous, and our reaching out is limited to others like ourselves, it still is a missional issue. We still need to cultivate great commission hearts!"

Dr. Manuel Ortiz

WHAT DOES A MULTIRACIAL CLASSIS LOOK LIKE?

The CRC is learning to live multiracially in other arenas as well. One of these is at the inter-congregational or classis level, what other traditions may call a district or a diocese. We'll look at two classes (the plural of classis is pronounced "class-ease").

Classis Hackensack

Classis Hackensack's claim to fame is New York City, one of the strategic gateways to the world. According to John Algera, pastor of Madison Avenue CRC in Paterson, New Jersey, nearly 25 percent of immigrants come into the United States through New York (second only to Los Angeles, with 27 percent). In response to this great mission opportunity, Classes Hackensack and Hudson have joined forces with the "Church of New York City's Multiplication Alliance" to plant 10,000 new churches in the New York City area in the next ten years. The CRC is committed to planting fifteen of them.

While the size and number of Hackensack congregations with predominantly white membership have sharply decreased, congregations consisting primarily or significantly of persons of color have increased dramatically. Of Hackensack's forty congregations, twenty-eight can be identified by their racial and ethnic diversity: one African-American, one African, one Chinese, one Filipino, six Hispanic, eleven Korean, and seven multiracial.

Diversity is even embedded into the vision statement. "It's our identity," said Andy Sytsma, pastor of Bridgeway Community Church in Haledon, New Jersey. The classis has done major restructuring, and its core leadership team is intentionally diverse. Andy Chun, Korean-American pastor to the predominantly white membership Covenant CRC in North Haledon, New Jersey, said, "I'm proud of the progress our classis has made."

Challenges

- *Changing traditions.* Classis leaders who are white still manage the business of classis, and tend to do so in traditional, church-orderly ways. According to Sheila Holmes, African American pastor of Northside Community Church in Paterson, New Jersey, "The culture of our Dutch brothers is to discuss papers and come to conclusions. Many of us from other cultures find it hard to get into and be a part of that process."

- *Limited resources.* As new congregations multiply, pastors of smaller, less affluent congregations often feel marginalized and isolated. Hispanic pastors say their members are not able to contribute financially the way Anglo members can. Others observed that when Home Missions grants conclude, local assistance is not enough to make up the difference.

Celebrations

- *Welcoming new pastors.* Since increasing the number of church plants, Hackensack now examines and welcomes at least two to four pastors at each meeting, with many requiring translation.

- *Relational growth.* On the eve of each classis meeting, the pastors gather for worship in various languages, sharing the Lord's Supper, and praying in pastoral cluster groups. Latino pastors emphasize the "family feel" and Korean pastors the "passion for prayer," according to Sytsma, resulting in "business becoming ministry."

Classis Greater Los Angeles

Similar to its East Coast counterpart, Classis Greater Los Angeles (GLA) includes forty-one congregations. Less than one-third of them (twelve) are predominantly white and the remaining twenty-nine congregations represent a rainbow of racial and cultural groups: three African American, one Chinese, three Filipino, five Hispanic, one Indonesian, eleven Korean, one Vietnamese, and four multiracial congregations.

In its early years, Classis GLA meetings were translated into Korean through headsets. "The language barrier was huge, and we knew the

"It doesn't feel like small, poor, minority churches like mine get much attention."
—Pastor Sheila Holmes

classes had to find a better way to serve our new Korean churches," said David Koll, pastor of Anaheim CRC. In 1996 the CRC established its first Korean-speaking classis, enfolding many first-generation Korean pastors into classis Pacific Hanmi.

Classis GLA desires to mix the cultures together and patiently learn from one another. "For the most part, there's a good spirit when we're all together—a love, growing respect, and unity among us," said Carl Kromminga, Jr., pastor of New City Church in Long Beach, California. Elmer Tandayu, pastor of Grace Filipino Church in Carson, California, agrees: "We are not just a body of CRC pastors and workers, but I can feel that we are one body in Christ."

Challenges

- *Chaos.* A classis of many cultures can feel like chaos sometimes, says Koll, which can cause conflicts or discomfort. "Some view chaos as a constant enemy, or that we've lost our sense of Reformed order. I think it's a good sign that we're being pushed out of our comfort zone."

- *Second-class.* Kromminga, whose congregation is predominantly African American, said the CRC continues to be too word-oriented, prizing its lengthy reports. "People who don't read or express themselves well in English step back and feel left out, like second-class citizens."

Celebrations

- *Enfolding.* In 2005 Koll led a multi-ethnic group of ten incoming pastors through an introductory curriculum prior to their classical examinations. Samuel Flores, Hispanic Ministries pastor at Rosewood CRC in Bellflower, California, said the group was more than a class to him, and helped him form partnerships across cultural

"We need to function more like family."
—Pastor Carl Kromminga, Jr.

lines. "We discovered that we felt similar attraction to the journey and convictions of this denomination, and that the CRC had an open door to 'foreigners' like us and our ideas," he said.

- *Project Timothy.* Classis GLA sponsors an annual leadership development camp for teens from diverse ethnic and racial backgrounds. Former campers are now returning as leaders and teaching younger students. "It's thrilling to get to the place where people who experienced the training are translating it into their own cultural lingo and passing it on to urban kids," said Kromminga. He is grateful that people are coming into leadership "who will contribute their unique way of doing business, until it doesn't look like 'our way' anymore but something better."

HOW DOES A MULTIRACIAL DENOMINATION BEHAVE?

Intentionality about being multiracial is important, not only for congregations and classes but also for the denomination and its ministries. Notwithstanding the CRC's isolationist beginnings, every chapter in its history reflects a deepening understanding of the mission of God—to reconcile all of alienated humanity through Jesus Christ.

Here are more recent signposts erected by synod itself:

- In 1988 synod began hosting multiethnic conferences, which included orientation and training for new pastors, many of whom were persons of color.

- In 1995 synod, recognizing its cultural whiteness, decided to appoint persons of color to serve as ethnic advisors to its annual meeting.

Estaban Lugo, appointed CRC
Race Relations Director in 2004

- In 1996 synod adopted a landmark report, "Biblical and Theological Principles for a Diverse and Unified Family of God." The report articulated twelve principles (summarized in Appendix A) and recommended implementation steps for the whole church. (This report is reproduced in the booklet *God's Diverse and Growing Family,* CRCNA 1996.)

- In 1999 synod affirmed the commitment of CRC agencies and institutions, as well as CRC congregations, to antiracism training and organizing, and to recruiting more persons of color for leadership roles.

- In 2004 synod declared, "Because the Christian Reformed Church's unity and diversity must mirror that of God, the Father, Son, and Holy Spirit, the members and agencies of the Christian Reformed Church are called to be reconciled with one another as a community of racially and ethnically diverse people of God" *(Acts of Synod 2004,* p. 558).

- In 2005 synod encouraged each classis to include at least one person of color in its annual four-person delegation to synod, beginning with Synod 2006.

WHAT DOES THIS HAVE TO DO WITH ME?

My experiences and observations over several decades, and, I believe, the convicting witness of the Holy Spirit, have led me to believe that the issue of race is the greatest mission challenge for the Christian church in North America in the twenty-first century.

The 1996 report "God's Diverse and Unified People" includes this profound declaration: "To be in Christ is in principle to be reconciled as a community of racially and ethnically diverse people, and that to ignore his calling to turn this principle into experienced reality is sinful according to God's Word and the Reformed confessions." If the apostle Paul were to show up in our segregated neighborhoods and single-culture congregations, I believe he would "oppose us to our face" (see Gal. 2:11).

> "To be in Christ is in principle to be reconciled as a community of racially and ethnically diverse people. . . ."
> —SYNOD 1996

The remarkable thing about new life in Christ is its all-encompassing transformation. "If anyone is in Christ he is a new creation . . ." (2 Cor. 5:17). "For all of you who were baptized into Christ have clothed yourselves with Christ. There is neither Jew nor Greek, slave nor free, male nor female, for you are all one in Christ Jesus" (Gal. 3:27-28).

Our relationship in Christ is more defining of who we are than our net worth, our nationality, our gender, or our race (Gal. 3:27). When we as African Americans or Asian Americans or European Americans or Latin Americans or Native Americans are baptized into Christ, our relationship in Christ is more central to our identity than anything else about us. South African missiologist David J. Bosch wrote, "Christ's work of reconciliation . . . leads to a new kind of body in which human relations are being transformed. In a very real sense mission, in Paul's understanding, is saying to people from all backgrounds, 'Welcome to the new community, in which all are members of one family and bound together by love'" (*Transforming Mission,* Orbis Books, 1999, p. 168).

God forever releases us from any notions of superiority or inferiority by revealing to us who we really are in Christ. As Jesus-followers we are all first and foremost children of God, and therefore first and foremost brothers and sisters of one another.

> We grieve that the church
> which shares one Spirit, one faith, one
>   hope,
> and spans all time, place, race, and
>   language
> has become a broken communion in a
>   broken world.
> When we struggle for the purity of the
>   church
> and for the righteousness God
>   demands,
> we pray for saintly courage.
> When our pride or blindness blocks
> the unity of God's household,
> we seek forgiveness.
> We marvel that the Lord gathers the
>   broken pieces
> to do his work,
> and that he blesses us still
> with joy, new members,
> and surprising evidences of unity.
> We commit ourselves to seeking and
>   expressing
> the oneness of all who follow Jesus.

—OUR WORLD BELONGS TO GOD, A CONTEMPORARY TESTIMONY, STANZA 43

DISCUSSION STARTERS

1. What do you find helpful about the proposed definition of a multiracial church?

2. Under what circumstances are you or others apt to feel like "outsiders" in your congregation?

3. What are some traditions or customs in the life of your congregation that are valued but not biblically required?

4. What are you willing to "sacrifice" to help your congregation become a more welcoming community to neighbors who are ethnically or racially different from you?

5. How much knowledge and understanding should incoming pastors from other traditions and cultures have of CRC history and the church order?

6. What are some unspoken assumptions behind the statement, "People of color are not going to change overnight, and white folks are not going to go away"?

APPENDIX A

BIBLICAL AND THEOLOGICAL PRINCIPLES FOR THE DEVELOPMENT OF A RACIALLY AND ETHNICALLY DIVERSE AND UNIFIED FAMILY OF GOD

CREATION

1. The world as God created it is rich and God-glorifying in its diversity.

2. The created world with all its diversity has its unity in the one God, who created it through Jesus Christ.

3. The unity and diversity of the human race and of created reality reflect the unity and diversity of the triune God (namely, his oneness and three-ness).

FALL

1. A fundamental effect of sin is the breakdown of community.

NEW CREATION

1. The uniting of all things in Jesus Christ is at the heart of God's eternal plan for the ages.

2. Reconciliation with God and reconciliation with one another are inseparable in God's saving work.

3. Already in the old covenant the scope of God's mission is racially and ethnically inclusive.

4. In Pentecost, the outpouring of the Holy Spirit upon the church, God gives new power to the church, power to break down walls of separation and create a community that transcends divisions of race, ethnicity, and culture.

5. The church is God's strategic vehicle for embodying, proclaiming, and promoting the unity and diversity of the new creation.

6. God calls Christians to find their deepest identity in union with and in the service of Jesus Christ.

7. Obedience in matters of racial reconciliation calls us, individually and corporately, to continually repent, to strive for justice, and to battle the forces of evil.

8. Christians live and work in the hope that one day the reconciliation of all things will be fully realized.

—Adopted by Synod 1996, CRCNA

APPENDIX B

KOREAN ETHNIC CHURCHES IN THE CRC

State or Province	City	Church Ministry	Date
Alaska	Anchorage	Alaska Korean CRC	1997
	Barrow	Barrow Korean Church	1996
Alberta	Edmonton	Edmonton So-Mang Church	1997
British Columbia	Kamloops	Kamloops Korean SoRang	2003
California	Alameda	Alameda Korean	2001
	Anaheim	Hanaro Church	2003
	Anaheim	Mission Community Church	
	Anaheim	Neung Ryuk Church	1987
	Anaheim	Sae Soon Dong San Church	2004
	Arcadia	Salt and Light Church	2001
	Artesia	New Hope Presbyterian	2003
	Burbank	Bethany Korean Community	2000
	Burbank	Los Angeles Global Church	2004
	Cerritos	Heaven Bound	1995
	Cerritos	Lord's Love Mission Church	1998

	Chatsworth	L.A. Peace Church	1998
	Covina	Bridge Church	2003
	Cypress	Hope of the World Church	2004
	Diamond Bar	SoMang Community	1993
	Diamond Bar	Body of the Lord	2000
	Downey	Faith Korean Presbyterian	
	El Cerrito	East Bay Korean	1991
	Fantana	New Joy CRC	2002
	Fountain Valley	K-A CRC of Orange County	1986
	Fullerton	City on a Hill	
	Fullerton	Faith Community Church	1993
	Fullerton	Garden Grove	1991
	Fullerton	Messiah Korean CRC	1978
	Fullerton	Orange Korean Church	
	Garden Grove	Orange Co. Calvary CRC	1998
	Garden Grove	Shema Presbyterian	2000
	Irvine	First Harvest Chapel	
	Irvine	Urim Church	1998
	Lake View Terrace	L.A. All Nations Church	2003
	Los Angeles	Greenfield Presbyterian	2000
	Los Angeles	Hokamsa Home Missions	2002
	Los Angeles	Joy Community Church	2004
	Los Angeles	Olympic Presbyterian	2004
	Los Angeles	The Gracious Ark	1988
	La Puente	Joy of Jesus CRC	2002
	Northridge	The Church of One Heart	2000
	Northridge	Valley in Christ Community	2001
	Northridge	Valley Dong San CRC	1992
	Norwalk	Spirit-Filled Church	1993
	Norwalk	Orange Han Min	1997
	Oxnard	Oxnard Korean Church	2003
	Reseda	San Bernardino Korean	1997
	Sacramento	Sacramento Pilgrim Church	1989
	Santa Clara	San Jose New Hope Church	2000
	Santa Clarita	Santa Clarita Valley Comm.	
	Santa Maria	Faith Korean Church of S.M.	2003
	Stevenson Ranch	Journey Christian Fellowship	2000
	Sunland	Chosen People CRC	1994
	Torrance	InAe Church	
	Westminster	Korean CRC of Orange Co.	1987
Colorado	Broomfield	Boulder Korean Church	
Florida	St Petersburg	Tampa Korean	1990
Hawaii	Honolulu	True Light Church	1994
Illinois	Wheeling	Chicago Reformed	1971
Iowa	Ames	Ames Korean/Campus	1988
Michigan	Ann Arbor	Ann Arbor Rock Church	
	Ann Arbor	Cornerstone CRC	2005

	Grand Rapids	Grace Korean CRC	
	Rochester Hill	Han Bit Korean CRC	1991
	Vicksburg	Kalamazoo Korean CRC	1987
	Wyoming	Grand Rapids Hahn-In	1985
Nevada	Las Vegas	L.V. Yung Kwang Church	1994
	Las Vegas	Somang PoDoWon	1989
New Jersey	Ambler	Elim Presbyterian	
	Clifton	Love Korean CRC	1997
	Livingston	Livingston Calvary Church	
	Ridgefield	Tree of Life Korean Church	2003
	Southampton	SungLim Presbyterian	2004
New Mexico	Albuquerque	Galilee Korean Presbyterian	1997
New York	Staten Island	New Life Community	2003
	Whitestone	East West Church of N.Y.	2003
Oregon	Clackamas	Zion Korean Church	2004
Pennsylvania	Blue Bell	Grace Community Chapel	
	Jenkinstown	Myung Sung Church	2002
Texas	Dallas	Dallas Great Light Church	
Virginia	Blacksburg	All Nations Fellowship	
Washington	Mill Creek	Seattle Dream Church	2004
	Federal Way	Kent First Korean CRC	1995
	Fife	Hebron Presbyterian CRC	1994
	Lynnwood	Vision Fellowship	1990
	Pacific	SumKiNun Church	
	Seattle	New Hope Korean	
	Spokane	Spokane Hope Presbyterian	1988
	Tacoma	Community Presbyterian	1990
	Tacoma	Puyallup Korean Church	2002

APPENDIX C

CRC ASIAN ETHNIC CHURCHES IN THE UNITED STATES AND CANADA (NOT INCLUDING CRC KOREAN-ETHNIC CHURCHES)

ASIAN AMERICAN
Bigelow, Minnesota, Asian-American CRC

CAMBODIAN
Holland, Michigan, Cambodian Fellowship
Stockton, California, Cambodian CRC
West Valley, Utah, Cambodian CRC

CHINESE
Abbottsford, British Columbia, Zion CRC
Chicago, lllinois, Hyde Park CRC
Denver, Colorado, Khmer CRC
Monterey Park, California, Chinese CRC
Richmond, British Columbia, Immanuel CRC
San Francisco, California, Golden Gate CRC
San Jose, California, Friendship Agape CRC

FILIPINO

Bellflower, California, Grace Filipino CRC
Carson, California, Grace Filipino CRC
Hayward, California, Living Faith Fellowship
Jersey City, New Jersey, Filipino CRC

HMONG

Grand Ledge, Michigan, Hmong CRC
Santa Ana, California, Mong CRC
Sheboygan, Wisconsin, Hmong CRC

INDONESIAN

Arcadia, California, Indonesian CRC

LAOTIAN

Brooklyn Park, Minnesota, North Center Lao CRC
Holland, Michigan, Lao Community CRC
New Brighton, Minnesota, New Life Lao CRC
Palmetto, Florida, St. Petersburg Laotian CRC
Sioux City, Iowa, Lao Unity CRC
Worthington, Minnesota, Lao CRC
Hamilton, Ontario, New Life CRC

VIETNAMESE

Kentwood, Michigan, Vietnamese Ref. Chr. Church
Moreno Valley, California, Laotian Vientiane CRC
San Jose, California, Liberty CRC
Westminster, California, Little Saigon CRC
Winfield, Illinois, Vietnamese New CRC

—SOURCE: CRC YEARBOOK 2005

APPENDIX D

CRC MULTIRACIAL CONGREGATIONS HONOR ROLL**

Location	Church Name	Start Date	Total Members
Bellflower, CA	Rosewood	1950	700
Bigelow, MN	Asian American	Emerging*	135
Chicago, IL	GAP Community	2002*	115
Chicago, IL	Loop Christian Ministries	1987*	65
Chicago, IL	Pullman	1980	249
Cleveland, OH	East Side	1872	149
Durham, NC	The River	1998*	NA
El Paso, TX	Sunshine Community	1976	142
Ewa Beach, HI	Anuenue Chr. Fellowship	1996*	120
Farmington, NM	Maranatha Fellowship	1962	106
Folsom, CA	River Rock	1998*	273

Gallup, NM	Bethany	1956	267
Grand Ledge, MI	Covenant	1980	84
Grand Rapids, MI	City Hope	1999*	75
Grand Rapids, MI	Coit Community	2002	131
Grand Rapids, MI	Grace	1962	490
Grand Rapids, MI	Madison Square	1970	1000
Grand Rapids, MI	Oakdale Park	1890	528
Grand Rapids, MI	Roosevelt Park Community	1994	434
Haledon, NJ	Bridgeway Community	2001	182
Hayward, CA	Christ's Community	1963	193
Holland, MI	Maple Avenue Ministries	1999	117
Kalamazoo, MI	Immanuel	1988	90
Long Beach, CA	New City	1993*	1988
Mangilao, Guam	Faith Presbyterian	NA	75
Miami, FL	South Kendall Community	1955	176
Monee, IL	Family of Faith	2001	205
Moreno Valley, CA	Oasis Community	1999	275
Nashville, TN	Faith	1983	105
Paterson, NJ	Madison Avenue	1910	205
Philadelphia, PA	Spirit & Truth Fellowship	1999	175
Sacramento, CA	The Gathering	2000*	NA
San Diego, CA	Trinity Fellowship	1993	65
Sunnyside, WA	Iglesia Evangelica	1999	75
Toronto, ON	All Nations Chr. Fellowship	2004	44
Toronto, ON	Friendship Community	1993*	40
Toronto, ON	Grace, Scarborough	1963	262
Vancouver, BC	First	1926	199
Washington, DC	Washington DC	1943	167
Williams Lake, BC	Cariboo Community	2001*	46
Zuni, NM	Zuni	1987	264

**Self-identified as multiracial congregations, that is, with no one racial group comprising more than 80 percent of the membership

*Indicates the date when worship services began, in the case of emerging churches.

—Source: CRC *Yearbook 2005*

APPENDIX E

CONTRIBUTOR BIOGRAPHIES

PROJECT LEADER

Al Mulder, baptized Alfred E., was born on a farm near Ireton, Iowa. He graduated from Calvin College in 1957 and Calvin Theological Seminary in 1960. He served three pastorates: in Luctor, Kansas; in a Home Missions ministry to Navajo students in Utah; and in Bethany Church, Gallup, New Mexico. From 1984 to 2003 Al was Home Missions director of new church development. He is the author of a study booklet, *Happiness Is . . .* and various articles on church planting and racial reconciliation. Al and his wife, Darlene, are members of Madison Square Church in Grand Rapids, Michigan.

Chapter 2

Harry Boonstra immigrated to North America from the Netherlands as a teenager in 1951. Upon their arrival in Canada, the Boonstra family joined a CRC of mostly Dutch-speaking immigrants—not unlike the congregations he describes in chapter 2. After earning his Ph.D. in English at Loyola University, Boonstra worked in the United States as a professor of English, as a theological librarian, and as an editor with Wycliffe Bible Translators. Dr. Boonstra was ordained as a minister in the CRC at age fifty. He has written and edited articles and books about Dutch emigration, church history, and worship.

Chapter 3

Louis M. Tamminga was born in the Netherlands. He came to Canada as a young man and later studied at Calvin College and Seminary. Rev. Tamminga has served congregations in Alberta, British Columbia, Iowa, and Ontario. From 1983 to 1995 he was director of CRC Pastor-Church Relations Services. He also served CRC World Missions as communications director and in ministering to missionaries abroad. Tamminga's writings include *Guiding God's People in a Changing World: a Handbook for Elders; The Empty Pew; On Your Way Rejoicing;* and other educational and inspirational materials.

Chapter 5

Reginald Smith was born and raised in Chicago. Reggie received his M.Div. degree from Calvin Theological Seminary in 1992 and was ordained in 1993 as a pastor at Northside Community CRC in Paterson, New Jersey. Since 1995 he has been senior pastor at Roosevelt Park Community CRC, a multiracial ministry in Grand Rapids, Michigan. He received a D.Min. degree from Western Theological Seminary in 2004. Dr. Smith enjoys life and ministry with his wife, Sharon, and their three daughters, Janelle, Katrina, and Mariah.

Chapter 6

Manuel Sergio Bersach was born in Cuba and came to the United States in 1969 by way of the Virgin Islands and Puerto Rico. Manny graduated from Covenant College and the Reformed Theological Seminary, and in 1987 was ordained in the Presbyterian Church in America. He was a missionary in Santiago, Chile, and a church planter in Miami, Florida. In 1999 Pastor Bersach and Piedras Vivas (Living Stones) Christian Church transferred from the PCA to the CRC. Bersach also chairs the local CRC Hispanic Task Force and is regional pastor for Classis Southeast USA.

Chapter 7

Edward W. Yoon grew up in a Presbyterian pastor's family and completed college and seminary in Korea. In 1985 he was married and ordained, both in Phoenix, Arizona. He obtained two additional masters' degrees and a D.Min. degree from Fuller Seminary. Dr. Yoon served several Korean American congregations; as a professor and president of Benjamin University in Commerce, California; and as a consultant to Korean small group ministry. He and his wife, Jenny, have three children: Michelle, David, and William. Dr. Yoon began a new pastorate in Phoenix in the fall of 2005.

Chapter 8

Mike Vander Pol was born in the Netherlands and immigrated to the United States at age fifteen. He met his wife, **Lois Vander Pol** (*nee* Warsen), a native of West Michigan, while attending Calvin College. Mike was ordained as a CRC minister after his graduation from Calvin Seminary. From there the Vander Pols ministered in cross-cultural settings in Honolulu, Taipei, San Francisco, and Manila—he as a missionary pastor and she as a teacher and school counselor. In their retirement the Vander Pols minister from their home base in Escondido, California.

CHAPTER 9

John VanTil says he was born a Calvinist with zest for life and love for all God's creation, but became a Christian after emigrating from the Netherlands to Canada at age eighteen. He returned to school and graduated from Calvin College and Seminary. Ordained in 1964, with Ellen (*nee* Van Harmelen) as his life partner, he was a church planter in Michigan and a campus pastor and longtime CRC Home Missions leader in Canada. In his "retirement" he is serving a new unaffiliated Chinese church in Toronto and as Ministry Developer for Classis Chatham.